TERRITORIAL CHANGES AND INTERNATIONAL CONFLICT

STUDIES IN INTERNATIONAL CONFLICT

Series Editor: Manus I. Midlarsky, Moses and Anuta Back Professor of International Peace and Conflict Resolution, Rutgers University

Volume 1: THE ONSET OF WORLD WAR
by Manus I. Midlarsky

Volume 2: WAR AND STATE MAKING
by Karen A. Rasler and William R. Thompson

Volume 3: PARADOXES OF WAR
by Zeev Maoz

Volume 4: THE PRICE OF POWER
by Alan C. Lamborn

Volume 5: TERRITORIAL CHANGES AND INTERNATIONAL CONFLICT
by Gary Goertz and Paul F. Diehl

TERRITORIAL CHANGES AND INTERNATIONAL CONFLICT

Gary Goertz
and
Paul F. Diehl

Studies in International Conflict
Volume 5

London and New York

First published 1992
by Routledge
11 New Fetter Lane, London EC4P 4EE

Simultaneously published in the USA and Canada
by Routledge
a division of Routledge, Chapman and Hall, Inc.
29 West 35th Street, New York, NY 10001

© Gary Goertz and Paul F. Diehl

Typset in 11 on 12½ Goudy by Falcon Typographic Art Ltd
Edinburgh & London
Printed and bound in Great Britain by
Biddles Ltd, Guildford and King's Lynn

All rights reserved. No part of this book may be reprinted or
reproduced or utilized in any form or by any electronic, mechanical or
other means, now known or hereafter invented, including photocopying and
recording, or in any information storage or retrieval system, without
permission in writing from the publishers.

Library of Congress Cataloging-in-Publication Data
Goertz, Gary, 1953–
Territorial changes and international conflict/
Gary Goertz, Paul F. Diehl.
p. cm. – (Studies in international conflict; v. 5)
Includes bibliographical references.
ISBN 0–415–07597–1
1. Territory, National.   2. Jurisdiction, Territorial.
3. International relations.   I. Diehl, Paul F. (Paul Francis)
II. Title.   III. Series.
JX4085.G56   1991
341.4'2—dc20
90–43715 CIP

British Library Cataloguing in Publication Data
Goertz, Gary
Territorial changes and international conflict.
(Studies in international conflict, v. 5).
1. Foreign relations   I. Title   II. Diehl, Paul F. (Paul Francis)
327.101
ISBN 0–415–07597–1

CONTENTS

List of Tables	*Page* ix
List of Figures	x
Acknowledgments	xi
CHAPTER 1 The Significance of Territory	1
CHAPTER 2 A Territorial History of the International System	33
CHAPTER 3 Entering International Society: Military Conflict and State Formation	57
CHAPTER 4 Exchanges of Homeland Territory Between States	81
CHAPTER 5 Territorial Changes and Recurring Conflict	105
CHAPTER 6 Territorial Changes and the Future	127
Appendix: Territorial Changes, 1816 to 1980	147
Bibliography	165
About the Authors	173
Index	175

LIST OF TABLES

Table 2.1	Regional Distribution of States, 1816 to 1980	Page 37
Table 2.2	Regional Distribution of Territorial Changes	46
Table 2.3	Nations with Greatest Involvement in Territorial Changes, 1816 to 1980	50
Table 2.4	Process of Territorial Change	54
Table 3.1	Regional Distribution of National Independences	61
Table 3.2	States Most Involved in Independence Cases	62
Table 3.3	Summary of Variables and Indicators	71
Table 4.1	Interstate Territorial Changes by Region and Century	84
Table 4.2	States Most Involved in Transfers of Homeland Territory	86
Table 4.3	Summary of Variables and Indicators	93
Table 4.4	Interstate Territorial Changes and Military Conflict, 1816 to 1913	95
Table 4.5	Interstate Territorial Changes and Military Conflict, 1914 to 1980	97
Table 5.1	Regional Distribution of Recurring Conflict	109
Table 5.2	Regional Distribution of Recurring Conflict, by Century	112
Table 5.3	States Most Involved in Recurring Conflict	113
Table 5.4	Summary of Variables and Indicators	120
Table 6.1	Remaining Dependent Territories	133
Table 6.2	Current Territorial Disputes	141

LIST OF FIGURES

Figure 2.1 Entries into the International System	Page 36
Figure 2.2 Population Added to the System	39
Figure 2.3 Area Added to the System	39
Figure 2.4 Nonindependence Changes in the System	41
Figure 2.5 Interstate Changes in the System	44
Figure 2.6 Area Changes in the System	45
Figure 2.7 Percentage of Major Power Changes	49
Figure 2.8 Percentage of Military Conflict Changes	51
Figure 3.1 Independences Over Time	60
Figure 3.2 Military Conflict and National Independence	63
Figure 3.3 LISREL Model of Military Conflict and National Independence	75
Figure 4.1 Military Conflict and Interstate Changes	87
Figure 5.1 Amount of Future Conflict	110
Figure 5.2 LISREL Model of Territorial Changes and Recurring Conflict	122

ACKNOWLEDGMENTS

There were a number of people and organizations that provided great assistance and encouragement in the preparation of this book. J. David Singer and the Correlates of War (COW) Project at the University of Michigan have provided much of the inspiration and empirical data upon which this book and our other work together are based. In particular, Philip Schaefer of the COW Project first collected and coded the data on territorial changes used here. He has our gratitude and respect as we frequently checked obscure parts of the data collection only to reaffirm Phil's original decisions. Additional data collection assistance came from Bouda Etemad and John O'Looney. Paul Bairoch allowed us to use some of his economic data and provided Gary with the proper intellectual environment at the Center for International Economic History at the University of Geneva to conduct serious empirical research. At various times, the Universities of Georgia, Geneva, and Illinois gave us strong institutional support and services. In particular, we would like to thank Merrily Shaw and Phyllis Koerner for helping prepare the final manuscript. A grant from the United States Institute of Peace helped us in the middle and latter stages of the research and we hope that organization is pleased with the result.

Once the manuscript was completed, Randolph Siverson and Harvey Starr reviewed the drafts and offered suggestions on how to sharpen our analysis. We profited from their suggestions and benefited greatly from their work on geopolitics as reflected throughout this book. Finally, Lisa Freeman, her able successor Lauren Osborne, and Manus Midlarsky provided great encouragement throughout the process. We are proud to include this book in their special series.

We wish to thank all those who helped us in this project and only hope that we can give reciprocal assistance in the future.

CHAPTER 1

The Significance of Territory

> . . . a voice cried out in him, a voice deeper than love cried out in him for his land. And he heard it above every other voice in his life . . . and when he was weary he lay down upon his land and he slept and the health of the earth spread into his flesh and he was healed of his sickness.
> —from Pearl Buck, *The Good Earth*

Humankind has always had a special relationship to the land on which it lives and which sustains it. In traditional societies, land was intimately tied to the local culture; gods were thought to inhabit particular areas, and important rites were held at specific locations. The transmission of culture from generation to generation meant the continuous inhabitation of the same land or geographic area. The decline of nomadic societies altered the relationship of humans to territory, but it did not diminish the importance of that relationship. Unlike other natural elements (such as air), land became a private good, not a public one: its use and enjoyment were open only to its owner. The creation of the concept of private property and the enclosure of the commons signaled changing political, economic, and social relationships. Paralleling this was the transfiguration of the private property of the prince or sovereign into a state or nation, exemplified by the creation of a distinction between the state's budget and the monarchy's household budget. This movement led to the concept of the "sovereignty of the people." The net result was the control of land by individuals at one level, and the domination and control of land by the state at a higher level. Individual land ownership even served as a prerequisite for the franchise—and thereby full membership—in some democratic societies. The exclusivity of property ownership is as evident by a No Trespassing sign on a neighbor's property as it was at the border between East and West Germany for so many years after World War II.

The roots of territorial conflict probably go beyond the beginning of recorded history. Humans first followed their animal instincts in marking off and defending areas of operation in the search for food and shelter. Organized societies then pursued similar practices as tribal groups fought with rivals for hunting grounds and villages. War, conceptualized as the organized exercise of military force by political groupings, dates to the onset of private property.[1] Man then sought to acquire and defend specific land areas that previously had been the common property of all nomadic peoples.

As humankind became more technologically advanced, the quest for territorial control seemed to take on greater proportions. The Roman Empire extended across Europe, Africa, and the Middle East in a successful attempt to control the Western civilized world. The most impressive acquisition of territory by an empire was that of the Mongols, whose control extended over almost all of Asia and well into Central Europe, all supervised by an army on horseback. In more recent times, attempts to control large and diverse land areas manifested themselves in colonialism and in England's pride that the sun never set on her empire. Even today, the ideological battle between the United States and the Soviet Union is often defined in geopolitical terms. Throughout history, there is a consistent link between territory and national power. Power is associated with demographic strength and economic resources that are generally related to land size.

Just as the desire for more territory has been a part of history, so too are the battles over this finite resource. It is difficult to think of a war that did not have some territorial component to it. Although the colonial wars of the eighteenth and nineteenth centuries were more explicitly over territory, the modern wars between India and Pakistan, as well as those in the Middle East, have territorial components tied to their religious and political roots. Yet it would be a mistake to characterize conflict over territory as inevitably leading to war. Many territorial disputes linger for years without either party feeling it necessary to use military force to pursue its claims. Indeed, it was over a hundred years before Argentina used military action to try to wrest control of the Falkland Islands from the British. Furthermore, some territorial exchanges are settled peacefully through a variety of nonviolent mechanisms; the Louisiana Purchase is but one example.

What we have set out to do in this work is to trace the changes in territorial control in the international system, with a special eye to identifying and explaining the military conflict that sometimes accompanies those changes. In this pursuit, we first direct our attention to the ways in which territory is linked to international conflict.

Territory and International Conflict

In seeking to understand the relationship between territory and war, there are several frameworks on which most works are based. Each of these frameworks starts with an overview of how geography affects international relations. Either implicitly or explicitly, one is then able to determine how geography affects the likelihood that any set of states will go to war. At one time, some scholars argued for geographic determinism, believing that a state's location, resources, and climate dictated what actions that state took. Recognizing that international behavior is a complex phenomenon, scholars no longer adopt such a determinist position. Here we identify three influential frameworks used to understand territory and war: those developed by Harold and Margaret Sprout, Kenneth Boulding, and Harvey Starr. Although they are related to one another, each has unique qualities. Furthermore, while each assigns a prominent role to geography, none contends that it plays a primary or exclusive role in the outbreak of war.

One of the most influential frameworks for analyzing international relations is the "ecological perspective" developed by the Sprouts.[2] According to their conception, international actions are conditioned by the environment or milieu that a given state faces. This environment includes demographics, technology, and resources, as well as geography. The Sprouts emphasize that states respond to their environment, but the environment does not compel policymakers to perform particular actions. Key variables are the decision-makers' assumptions about, or perceptions of, the environment. It is this interaction between man and his environment that affects the international actions chosen by a state. Overall, the environment poses some limitations on possible actions taken by a state. The Sprouts coined the term "environmental possibilism" to describe how the milieu can enhance or inhibit the ability of a state to act.

With respect to geography and war, the Sprouts' framework suggests that geography does not dictate that war occur between two states. Indeed, it might be said to be only one of several factors that constitute the environment in which states decide to use military force or not. Nevertheless, the location, size, climate, and natural resources of a state are a function of its geography. Correspondingly, some actions are less feasible because of those characteristics. For example, a state may be unable to launch an air strike against an opponent if that enemy is thousands of miles away and the attacker has no refueling capacity for its air force. An isolated country may find it easier to defend itself than one that shares many borders with hostile nations. According to the ecological perspective, geography is one of many influences that define the possibilities for war.

In his framework, Boulding notes that states vary in their ability to affect circumstances in certain areas; he labels these as zones of viability.[3] In some areas, a state is unconditionally viable, while in others the degree of influence is either more constrained or nonexistent. Boulding believes that there is a strong geographic dimension in the delineation of these zones. States are thought to be most viable in the areas in which they have sovereignty, and less viable as they move farther from their home base. Accordingly, he postulates a "loss-of-strength gradient" that is the degree to which a state's military and political power diminishes as the state attempts to influence other states and events farther away from its home base. For example, the ability of the United States to carry out the Grenada invasion was much easier than the aborted hostage rescue mission in Iran, in part because of the ease of logistics given the proximity of Grenada to the United States.

The loss-of-strength gradient has at least two implications for the relationship of geography to war. First, great distances impose constraints on the policy options available to decision-makers. This seems to be consistent with the notion of environmental possibilism advanced by the Sprouts. States are inherently constrained by geographic limitations in the selection of policy options, including the decision to go to war. Second, beyond a reaffirmation of the Sprouts' analysis, Boulding's concept also has implications for the decision calculus of policymakers. Although geography may eliminate many possibilities from the "menu of choice" for policymakers, many still remain. Yet, even though many courses of action are still possible, geographic factors may make the odds of success for some actions better than others. For example, geographic location may hinder, although not prevent, a state's ability to retaliate against a distant opponent. In this case, that state may decide not to undertake the action because the risks of failure are too great; geography thus affects the desirability of some options. A state's power depends on the geographic distance between the home state and the potential war opponent. A great distance may be outweighed by a preference for military force by the state or by the risk-taking propensity of its leadership. Thus, geography influences not only the possibility for conflict, but also the likelihood it will be chosen as an option by a decision-maker.

Starr derives his concepts of "opportunity" and "willingness" from the frameworks of Boulding and the Sprouts.[4] Starr's framework is the most developed of the empirical work on geography and war over the last decade, mainly because the work on borders and war by Starr and his colleagues Most and Siverson has formed the centerpiece of that literature. Starr defines opportunity as the "possibility of interaction between entities or behavioral units of some kind."[5] Thus, opportunity is similar to the concept of environmental possibilism put forward by the Sprouts and to the idea of a decision-making "menu" advanced by Russett.[6] It is also related to the concept of viability advanced by Boulding. The central assumption is that the greater the opportunity for a given action or event, the more likely, ceteris paribus, it will occur.

The second component of the framework, willingness, refers to the desirability of the decision option to the policymaker. As Starr notes, willingness relates to "the processes by which (decision-makers) *recognize opportunities* [emphasis in original] and then, given these opportunities, become willing to choose war as a behavioral alternative."[7] Once again, Starr has returned to the original framework of the Sprouts, this time to point out the importance of perception as decision-makers interact with their environment. Most discussions of deterrence implicitly analyze the willingness factor.

In Starr's formulation, there must be opportunity and willingness before there can be a decision for war; in effect, opportunity and willingness are necessary but not sufficient conditions for war. It should be noted that there are several dimensions to each of these conditions, geography being only one of them. In addition, opportunity and willingness are not necessarily separate in the decision to go to war. Most commonly, the opportunity to engage in war may enhance the willingness of the decision-maker to choose that option. For example, the ease of trade between neighboring states because of their numerous interaction opportunities may enhance the willingness of both sides to continue or expand such arrangements. Thus, opportunity and willingness are multidimensional and potentially interrelated concepts.

Territorial concerns are important parts of opportunity and willingness, according to Starr's framework.[8] Geographic conditions, such as shared borders or proximity, influence the interaction opportunities available to states. States close to each other interact more than those apart. Geographic factors may allow states to come in contact with one another, allowing for more conflict or cooperation opportunities. Geographic proximity may also provide the occasion for neighboring states to become involved. Like the Sprouts', Starr's framework posits that geography is only one factor affecting the opportunities for interaction and conflict. Furthermore, this framework treats geography as a conditioning variable, affecting only the possibility for conflict; in this way, geographic determinism is again rejected.

Although geography would seem to have more relevance in affecting opportunities, it also has some impact on the willingness of states to engage in war. Geography can affect the structure of risks and opportunities that influence the decision calculus of policymakers. The geographic proximity or strategic importance of an opponent or ally may make a given state more or less willing to attack or defend that opponent or ally. Here, Starr notes again the influence that relative opportunity can have on the willingness of a state to act.

With these frameworks in mind, one can classify the impact that territory or geography has on interstate conflict into two broad categories: as a facilitating condition for conflict and as a source or subject of conflict.

TERRITORY AS A FACILITATING CONDITION

In considering the regional dispersion of war, it becomes evident that some areas of the world have experienced comparatively less war than others.[9] Europe, in particular, has been relatively immune from war in the period after 1945. This variation in war across space suggests a strong geographic dimension to the outbreak and escalation of conflict.

Wesley posited that the frequency of war was a function of geographic opportunity.[10] Although most scholars are unwilling to accept that geography is the only factor in the equation for opportunity or that opportunity alone will produce war, a number of researchers have started from Wesley's premise. One of the key variables thought to determine geographic opportunity is the number of shared borders that a state possesses. Just as an individual is more likely to be shot by a member of his or her own family than a stranger because of increased interactions and opportunities, states are believed to experience more conflict with their neighbors than with other states. Early research by Richardson suggested that the more borders a state had, the more likely it was to experience conflict and war.[11] The existence of a border increases the number of interactions between those actors that share the border and hence the opportunity for serious conflict. By this logic, actions taken in one state are more likely to affect its neighbors as new economic policies in El Salvador did to Honduras prior to the Football War.[12] The peaceful existence of Australia and New Zealand is often attributed to the absence of land borders and relative geographic isolation.

Starr and Most offer a broader view than Richardson's simple concept that more interactions lead to conflict.[13] They suggest that borders do not cause war, but rather structure the risks and opportunities in which conflicting behavior is more likely to occur. They argue that proximate nations will be perceived as more threatening than those that are farther away, because distant states are less viable than proximate ones. Starr and Most also point out that states with many borders confront a security dilemma because they face many potential aggressors whose power is not offset by distance. For major powers, the border effect is weaker, perhaps because major powers tend to be surrounded by relatively weak neighbors; major powers may find it easier to deter such neighbors and may use means other than military force to influence those states successfully. A later study confirms these effects for the African continent.[14]

Another, related argument is that the greater the number of borders a state has, the more uncertainty that state faces.[15] The next inferential step is that uncertainty increases a state's propensity for war. Although it is difficult to dispute that a greater number of borders increases uncertainty, that uncertainty leads to war has been a debatable proposition in the literature on international conflict.[16] In general, however, this assertion is consistent with Starr and Most's contention that geography has an impact on the structure of risks and opportunities that confront a state.

Diehl has investigated major power rivalries of the last 150 years and found that contiguity to the site of the dispute for one side was a virtual necessary condition for escalation to war.[17] Instead of shared borders with a state, the facilitating condition was geographic proximity to an area in dispute (that is, where the war would take place). In explaining the findings, he agrees with Starr and Most in that the opportunity for conflict is greater for states closer to home. In addition, however, the willingness of states to fight is also enhanced by geographic proximity. States may be more willing to fight over events or issues that are closer to home because they are considered more important than those farther away. Furthermore, the loss of strength gradient will make decision-makers less willing to fight great distances away from their home base. Thus, territorial proximity influences both the opportunity and willingness of states to enter war.

Closely related to the impact of shared borders on the outbreak of war is the *diffusion effect* resulting from geographic proximity.[18] It is geography's role in the diffusion or spread of conflict that has fostered the most attention in the scholarly literature in the past decade, again in part because of the work of Starr and his colleagues. What is known in anthropology as Galton's problem[19] is in this context the possibility that conflicts are not *independent* events across time and space. For example, conflict in one state may lead to conflict occurring in another state.

In a series of articles, Starr and Most have looked at the possibility of positive and negative spatial diffusion of war—the war involvement of one state affects the likelihood that another state will become involved in war.[20] In particular, they posit that war spreads when there is a large number of interactions between the states; as noted above, shared borders are the means by which the number of interactions is increased. They first tested whether having a bordering state that is at war increases the propensity for a state subsequently to be at war itself. Using three different data sets, Starr and Most found that a state with a warring neighbor was three to five times as likely to be at war as one that did not have a bordering state at war. They argue that "warring borders" increase uncertainty and decrease the degree of control that states have in a given area and therefore increase the prospects for war. The spread of the Vietnam War into Cambodia and the spillover of the Soviet-Afghan conflict into Pakistan are notable examples.

In later works, Starr and Most attempt to extend the analysis to one region, Africa, seeking to discover if the same relationship holds on a regional as well as a global level. First, they discover that the results found in Africa are generally similar to those found on the global level, with some differences across time, and that noncolonial borders have a greater impact in the latter part of the 1960 to 1977 time period. More precisely, they find that interactions as indicated by noncolonial borders are more strongly related to conflict than are colonial border interactions and the effect is enhanced if the borders are land instead of sea borders. The type of war (internal or external) does not seem to affect the diffusion across borders. Finally, when war did spread across borders, the warring border nations were not necessarily the opponents of the state in question nor did that state become more likely to join the ongoing conflict—it was just as likely to be involved in a new war.

As in southern Africa, many protagonists base their troops in neighboring states, causing the military fighting to spill across national boundaries. States may also take advantage of their neighbors' preoccupation with a war to seize a piece of disputed territory or attack another state in the area; Libya's attempts to take portions of northern Chad during that country's civil unrest attest to this motivation. Finally, contacts between states, the result of the ease of communication and transportation across neighboring states, may induce conflict of similar varieties or prompt intervention by a concerned neighbor. The alleged "domino effect" in Southeast Asia, which served as one justification for United States intervention in Vietnam, is another way of describing the spread of conflict to neighboring territories.

Starr and Most's work on diffusion from geographic proximity parallels their analysis on the impact of shared borders; the theoretical explanations for both effects are similar, focusing on interaction opportunities and the role of uncertainty. The difference is that in the case of diffusion, geographic proximity allows the spread of existing war or conflict in some cases, and the border effect does not rely on concurrent or previous conflict for war to occur. In the Richardsonian formulation, one can presume that the conflict involves those who share the border, whereas diffusion effects mean that the conflict also affects other states in the same geographic area.

Much of the other scholarly literature on diffusion has relied on an analogy between the spread of war and the spread of disease.[21] It is not surprising that the terms *contagion* or *infection* are often used. Before one can catch a disease, one must have some contact with an infected person. A similar argument is made with a state and its exposure to war. Proximity is then an important condition for the transmission of the war disease. Appropriately, not all studies of diffusion concentrate primarily or exclusively on the territorial component; there are several other factors that may play a role in the spread of conflict. Yet, geography has been an important concern in several studies. Davis, Duncan, and Siverson analyze dyadic war and conclude that war is primarily contagious (as opposed to addictive) and that the key variable in the spread of war is interaction opportunities, which foreshadows much of the later analysis by Starr and Most.[22]

Other diffusion studies look at geography as a parameter that conditions how far war can spread. Implicitly, geographic proximity is again the critical component in determining which states will be affected by the conflict. The spread of war occurs primarily within regions, not across regions.[23] In particular, however, there is apparently a much greater effect in Europe than in any other region.[24] This again suggests that geographic distance is a limiting condition. Outbreaks of war in specific regions are not related to outbreaks in other parts of the international system.

Houweling and Siccama argue that the spread of war must

consider not only a spatial or geographic component, but also a temporal one.[25] They identify the interaction of the spatial and temporal components as the key to understanding the spread of conflict. They also find that diffusion is confined primarily to certain geographic regions. Yet, rather than cite interaction opportunities, Houweling and Siccama believe that the effect of war on the power distribution between states is more likely to affect the chances for the diffusion of war. Because war is likely to have a greater impact on the power distribution on a regional level, rather than a global one, the diffusion effects are confined to that region. The Chinese decision to "punish" Vietnam for its Cambodian incursion is no doubt related to this occurrence. They also note that different regions have different patterns of diffusion, with the Western Hemisphere experiencing the least, and Europe the most over the last 165 years. The influence of the United States and the Monroe Doctrine may be responsible for arresting the spread of conflict in the former. One might suggest that the small land area of Europe, together with a large number of shared borders, may account for the effects in the latter. Diffusion patterns also change over various historical periods.

From the studies of territory as a facilitating condition of war, we can derive several conclusions. First, geography is one of several factors that structure the risks and opportunities that a state faces. A shared border increases the interaction opportunities that a state has with another state, perhaps increasing the prospects for hostilities between the two. Geographic proximity to the site of a dispute may also make a state more willing and able to fight a war. Second, for many of the same reasons, shared borders and geographic proximity are important factors in the diffusion of conflict. The likelihood of war in one country or region is enhanced if there is a neighboring state at war.

Territory facilitates the initiation and diffusion of conflict, but a third finding is that this effect is not necessary for the outbreak of war. There are potentially several other facilitating conditions for conflict that may enhance, supersede, or have effects independent of those from geography. One possibility is that alliances increase (by drawing allies into a conflict) or decrease (through deterrence) the spread of conflict even among geographically proximate states. Most, Schrodt, Siverson, and Starr look at the effects of borders and alliances in the diffusion of conflict.[26] They find that both alliances and borders play important roles in the diffusion of conflict. Beyond multiple factors in the equation, there are significant differences across different regions and time periods. This suggests that the relationship between geography and war is not uniform and that various other factors may account for those differences.

TERRITORY AS A SOURCE OF CONFLICT

Beyond merely facilitating conflict, territory can be a source of conflict as states struggle over its control. At one time, scholars focused almost exclusively on the quest of major powers to acquire strategic areas of the globe in order to enhance military and economic opportunity. The prescriptive notions of a "Rimland" or "Heartland" are consistent with this kind of focus.[27] It was thought by some that control over certain areas of the European continent was a necessary and sufficient condition for preeminence in world affairs. Since no state achieved such control, it is difficult to assess the validity of such claims. Yet, since the time of these models, there has been a greater recognition that conflict over territory occurs for more than strategic reasons and involves more than just the major powers of the world.

States still seek to control areas of the globe for strategic purposes, as the Soviet domination of Eastern Europe attests. Nevertheless, territorial issues have come to mean much more. As noted below, territorial conflict may result from the importance of territory for economic, political, historical, and ethnic reasons. Furthermore, battles over territory are not confined to major powers in the world. In earlier eras, imperial/colonial powers were the primary combatants in the quest for territorial control. Since World War II, however, it is predominantly the smaller states that have been involved in territorial issues and conflict in general. All but a few wars in the last 45 years have involved at least one minor state, and many of these wars, such as the Ethiopia-Somalia War, have been confined to small states battling over territorial issues.

Despite the apparently salient concern of territorial disputes, scholars have devoted relatively little attention to this subject matter in the past few decades. This is not to say that scholars have not been concerned with territorial issues and geography. The preceding review of studies illustrates this point. Rather, studies of diffusion and borders have not been concerned with states fighting over competing territorial claims. Such studies do not look to the sources or bases of the dispute (that is, the territory), but instead focus only on how the territory and its characteristics (for example, proximity) affect decisions for war.

The work that has been done is primarily the product of research by geographers and historians. Although often insightful, these works are largely descriptive, single case studies without a broad theoretical outlook. There are several explanations for this paucity of work. First, it is evident that a disproportionate amount of conflict research is focused on major powers and the superpowers in particular. Some of this can be attributed to the ethnocentric concerns of the large number of American scholars who work in this area. Yet, scholars also look at major powers because the actions of these states exercise the greatest impact on the international system and its political processes. As noted above, however, territorial disputes frequently do not involve major powers, and even less frequently involve major powers on both sides of the dispute; thus, not surprisingly, attention is not directed to these situations. Although territorial concerns are not irrelevant to issues of deterrence and the like, they are relegated to the back seat in the analyses of the superpower rivalry.

An ignorance of territorial issues is more than the product of a major power bias in conflict research. In many ways, it is a reflection of a deliberate research strategy in the study of conflict processes. Most conflict research has ignored the issues and their salience involved in a given dispute. Instead, scholars have relied on variations in the attributes of the states involved or attributes of the international system to explain the initiation and escalation of conflict. In effect, they have relied on such factors as alliances, the power distribution, arms races, and the presence of third parties to predict and explain conflict. What the states are fighting over and how salient the dispute is to the participants are not considered.

The strategy of focusing only on national and systemic attributes is consistent with a realpolitik world view. In that scheme, all actions are done to enhance power and it does not matter what particular issues are involved. Furthermore, states are believed to act similarly in making decisions to use military force, regardless of how one side or the other might view the significance of the territory in dispute (except as it affects national interests). The above analysis might suggest that this approach is fatally flawed. In fact, the strategy has been reasonably successful. Various research enterprises, such as the Correlates of War Project and the Dimensions of Nations Project, to name two, have made significant progress in isolating the conditions for conflict and its escalation. Yet, we believe that in order to build on this work, scholars must extend their analyses to include a consideration of the issues and their importance in disputes between states.

With respect to territorial disputes, we believe that much of their importance or salience is attributable to the characteristics of the territory itself. It is the value of the territory in dispute that may be one of the keys for assessing when states will fight and when they will resolve their differences peacefully. If beauty is in the eye of the beholder, then the value of a given piece of territory also varies according to the perceptions of the state or states involved in a dispute. Nevertheless, we believe that certain characteristics of territory can be recognized as valuable regardless of whose perspective is considered. These characteristics are what we call the intrinsic importance of territory. In contrast, the relational importance of a territory is made up of characteristics that have different degrees of significance for different states; in effect, a territory might be considered extremely valuable by one state and yet not at all important by another state depending on these attributes. Below, we explore the characteristics of intrinsic and relational importance in seeking to identify the value that territory holds for states in the international system.

INTRINSIC IMPORTANCE

The first attribute of a territory that might be considered part of its intrinsic importance is its natural resource base: the availability and control of minerals, energy sources, and water. In earlier times, primacy was placed on the accessibility of the ocean because trade and military power were largely determined by naval capability; correspondingly, territory on the sea or with connecting waterways was considered valuable. Although access to port facilities is still an important concern, greater emphasis is now placed on mineral and other resources in a territory. Control over significant oil reserves can permit leverage over other states' economies as the 1973 oil embargo demonstrated. The repeated statements by the Carter and Reagan administrations that the Persian Gulf area is of vital interest to the United States indicates that even sand covered territory thousands of miles away can be considered important to all states.

It can be pointed out that states may not always recognize the intrinsic importance of a territory in terms of its natural resources. Estimates of resource reserves have been notoriously inaccurate,[28] and it is doubtful whether states have a good idea of the true value of a territory when they decide to acquire or relinquish sovereignty over it. "Seward's icebox" was a joke in the nineteenth century, but the acquisition of Alaska provided the United States with one of the largest oil reserves in the world, including significant gold deposits, that led to an end to such jokes. Beyond some uncertainty associated with the resource value of a territory, there is the difficulty in extracting those resources. If a state is unable to take advantage of the natural resources within its borders, then some of the value of that territory is lost. Both the inability to detect and extract natural resources have been mitigated with advances in technology and the passage of time.

Nevertheless, while the resource base of a country is a component of a territory's intrinsic importance, it must be recognized that the objective presence of those resources is not always proof that the territory will be immediately perceived as having great value.

The conflict that occurs over resources takes place not only as a result of the simple desire to own those resources, but also the desire to control the allocation of those resources. Many times states are upset with the distribution or principles of distribution of those resources.[29] Controlling the land area is one solution to a situation in which access to vital raw materials is restricted; scenarios for United States military action in the Middle East are often predicated on the interruption of the oil flow.

Territorial sovereignty also provides markets for the controlling state. New land areas offer not only sources of raw materials, but also the ability to sell the products made from those raw materials to the populace of the new territory. The colonial expansionism that was prevalent among major powers for centuries was partially rooted in this motivation. One could offer different interpretations, mercantilist or Marxist, of such actions, but the underlying desire for more territory is a part of the market strategy of both. It remains a debatable point, however, whether the British Empire was in fact a paying proposition or not.

A mercantilist strategy dictates that states acquire land at their periphery in order to derive the market benefits and resources that accompany control over that territory. The net flow of financial capital should ultimately favor the home state at the expense of the peripheral area. A Marxist interpretation of this situation is not dramatically different, although it carries stronger normative overtones. In particular, Lenin argued that capitalist states must expand their territorial holdings in order to survive.[30] Domestic overproduction and market saturation necessitate that new markets external to the state itself be found.[31] New markets are achieved by the acquisition of colonial and other subjugated territories. Conflict over territorial, and therefore market and resource, control occurs under two scenarios. First, capitalist states compete among each other for control over colonial territory. The Fashoda Crisis in 1898 between Britain and France can be cited as an example of this kind of rivalry. Second, conflict arises when the inhabitants of the peripheral areas seek independence and national self-determination. The resulting battles carried out in Vietnam and Algeria against French rule, for example, stem from this motivation.

A third intrinsic value of territorial control is the land itself. A fertile area could greatly enhance the food production or export capacity of the state that rules it. The Chaco region in South America provided important economic opportunities for Paraguay and Bolivia; the dispute was significant enough to precipitate one of the rare interstate wars in the Western Hemisphere during this century. Land also has more than agricultural and economic potential. It can provide the space needed for economic development and expansion. The Nazis' quest for *Lebensraum* is indicative of the territorial component that can comprise national development. Control over land area may also be critical in the development of the state. Elias hypothesizes that control over trade routes for taxation purposes was critical in the formation of the modern European state.[32]

When a state assumes sovereignty over a land area, it also gains some control over the people living in that territory. This can be a tremendous benefit if the population is large and the working age citizens are educated and skilled. Such a population can assist in economic development by permitting advanced economies of scale as well as offering the prospect for a mass army with a minimum of economic dislocation. Until quite recently, a state's productive capacity was directly proportional to the size of its population. A large population seems to be a necessary, but not a sufficient, condition for attainment of major power status. France's relatively small population compared to her European rivals was a consistent military and economic disadvantage especially as she tried to meet the challenge of a unified Germany in the late nineteenth and early twentieth century. Additional territory may provide the population resources needed to meet challenges from rivals.

Part of a territory's intrinsic value lies not in its physical components, but in the opportunities made possible by its possession. The control over a piece of territory can expand the number and variety of opportunities available to a state. Trade opportunities may be enhanced because of the closer proximity of production to potential markets; the additional resources and markets from that territory could also assist trade opportunities. Prospects for military or political intervention could also be increased because states may have greater interest in an area and may have the ability to threaten or use military force there.

RELATIONAL IMPORTANCE

There are other characteristics of territories that make control over them especially important to some countries. These characteristics are only apparent when they are considered in relation to the state involved in the territorial dispute. What may be considered a vital aspect of the territory to one state may not be particularly important to its rival. Nevertheless, states often place as much or more value on these relational characteristics than on the intrinsic value of a given territory.

The first characteristic of a territory's relational importance is its geographic location relative to a given state. All things being equal, the closer a piece of territory is to a state's homeland, the more significant it will become for that state. Areas close to home, and especially those directly bordering one's homeland, will be viewed as more vital to security interests than those much farther away. A hostile state is viewed as more threatening when it is next door than when it is half way around the world. The Soviet Union's reaction to the possible loss of a friendly government in Afghanistan was swift and dramatic—a military invasion. The Soviet reaction to the fall of the Allende regime in Chile was much more subdued. In part, this is attributable to the relative geographic proximity of each state to the Soviet homeland. A similar difference in reaction is evident from the United States response to new socialist regimes in Nicaragua and Mozambique in the late 1970s.

States appear more eager to fight for a territory closer to home than they are for a distant territory. Evidence indicates that almost all major power wars in the last 175 years began when the dispute site was directly contiguous to one of the parties.[33] This demonstrates that even though states may desire territorial control at many locations, they may only be willing to fight for those close to home. A territory may be particularly important to a state because of its peculiar security needs or history. Troops and weapons in the Polish corridor are of special concern to the Soviet Union because of the history of invasions through that passage. The Israeli preoccupation with the Golan Heights is rooted in that area's strategic military location.

Beyond the decreased value that states attach to territories distant from their homeland, there is also a decreased ability to press claims at great distances. The logistical difficulties in fighting a distant war combined with the negative impact on troop morale provide a distinct "home field" advantage.[34] The American experience in the Vietnam War is an oft-cited example of this effect. The geographic distance to the locus of conflict must play a role in decision-makers' calculations of potential success. Thus, the importance of acquiring a given territory, as well as the ability to do so, are related to the geographic distance of that territory to the state in question.

Some may argue that distance is no longer relevant in an advanced technological age when weapons can destroy targets across continents. It is undeniable that advances in communication and transportation have decreased effective distances between countries. Yet, even among the superpowers, territorial concerns are still important. The deployment of nuclear weapons anywhere in the world is considered threatening, but it was deployments in Cuba and Europe that have prompted crises or serious tensions; nuclear weapons in close proximity to the superpowers are a powerful symbol of the threat of atomic destruction as well as a complication to strategic planning in that the warning times for attack are cut by at least two-thirds. Furthermore, despite technological advances, the United States maintains military bases around the world to offset the constraints imposed by the geographic distance between the American homeland and potential targets of military action. For a Third World country, the geographic limits of its security concerns may extend no farther than its immediate border areas.

Another dimension of a territory's relational importance is the ethnic composition of its populace. States may believe that they have a claim on a given area because they share a common race, religion, or national origin with the population of the disputed territory. Thus, the unification of Austria and the Suedetenland into the Third Reich was considered an immediate goal for Nazi Germany, whereas control over less important areas in Asia and Africa were left to German allies. Clearly, the value of the territory varies tremendously depending on the relative similarity between the ethnic heritages of a given territory's population and those of a state.

Part of the origin of such territorial conflict stems from the creation of state boundaries that do not correspond to national or ethnic boundaries.[35] In some cases, boundaries divide homogeneous groups into separate sovereignties; China, Korea, and Germany are the most obvious examples. In other instances, ethnically heterogeneous groups are forced to unite in the same state; many African states fit this pattern. Whichever the case, states may regard such boundaries as artificial and seek to reunite groups with the same ethnic heritage. The war between Ethiopia and Somalia in the late 1970s is consistent with this irredentist motivation.

Related to ethnic considerations, a territory may have historical importance to a particular state. This could be the result of economic or political connections in the past or some common experience that was shared (for example, a common colonial heritage). The Israeli annexation of the West Bank was rooted in its historical claim that the area was part of the ancient Jewish homeland. Some in Syria regard Lebanon as a part of "Greater Syria" and hence an area that should be dominated or controlled by Syria. Historical claims are common in territorial disputes, but they are rarely given any weight in international law; this should not imply, however, that such considerations are not important in the decisions of individual states.

A given territory may have little economic value, but in a specific situation, that territory may take on great importance in the eyes of the disputants because of its history, location, or population characteristics. Throughout this analysis, the implication has been that territorial acquisition is desirable. Indeed, there is strong evidence to suggest that territorial control offers the benefits that accrue from the tangible and intangible assets accompanying it. Yet, not all territorial acquisition is beneficial to the sovereign. An area may be rich in a strategic mineral, yet complicate a state's ability to defend itself. Although one normally thinks of a large population as a contribution to national power, it can also pose problems of integration and political control to the state, as in India. An addition of unproductive numbers of individuals to a population could strain available resources and harm the economy. The transfer of any area of the Sahel in Africa, and the corresponding famine and starvation, to another state might be regarded as an economic benefit to the yielding state and a burden to the new sovereign. Furthermore, extensive territorial holdings and commitments may draw attention and resources (especially those needed for defense) away from the maintenance of a major power's global network.[36] In effect, too much territory can have negative returns in the long run; territorial acquisition may resemble an investment curve that entails diminishing, and eventually negative, returns at specified points.

Recognizing the paucity of previous research on territorial conflict and the need to consider the intrinsic and relational importance of territory in decisions to use military force, this book concerns itself with identifying the conditions under which military conflict over territory occurs. There are three problem areas that are the centerpiece of studies on territory as a source of conflict. These are state-formation conflicts, interstate conflicts, and recurring conflict. In looking at these areas, we believe that this investigation can reveal additional theoretical insights into the processes underlying territorial disputes. In this way, we can identify when states will be born through violent territorial disputes, when they will fight over territory, and when that violence will repeat itself over time. At present, the theoretical understanding of territorial conflict is primarily anecdotal and not distinct from the general understanding of international conflict. In the following sections, we review those areas and identify what prior research has reported about the conditions for military conflict in each set of cases. Each will be a subject of investigation in a subsequent chapter of this book.

STATE-FORMATION CONFLICTS

The first area is territorial disputes in the context of state formation. Among the legal requirements of statehood is the effective occupation and control of a defined land area. For a people seeking independence, the achievement of this requirement can be a violent process. The road to Algerian and other states' independence was a bloody one as imperial/colonial powers resisted relinquishing control of those areas. In other instances, such as Italy and Germany, the process of unification into a modern state was also achieved through the use of military force. Yet, it must be recognized that the process of achieving independence is not always a violent one. Many states have achieved their independence through peaceful means. Many African states became independent in the 1950s and 1960s when their imperial/colonial masters voluntarily transferred sovereignty. Why are some territorial disputes that involve soon-to-be formed states violent, while others are resolved peacefully?

Part of the equation affecting the chances for military conflict in the national independence process apparently lies in the characteristics of the imperial/colonial power. In particular, whether the imperial/colonial power is in a period of ascendancy or decline at the time of independence has an effect on the likelihood of military conflict; such conflict may be more likely in the period of decline. As its power decreases, the imperial/colonial state may fight to maintain its empire and concurrently the indigenous dependent population may believe that the imperial/colonial master is more vulnerable to attack. Furthermore, the period of ascendancy for the imperial/colonial power should be a time when territories are acquired, not lost. One might also expect that any challenges to the existing order then would either be defeated or resolved with the consent of the imperial/colonial power.

The "long cycle" framework[37] posits that various wars, including those that involve national independence, occur in the periods of "delegitimation" and "deconcentration" when the hegemon finds its power on the wane. Doran and Parsons note a similar result when a major power passes through a period of decline.[38] At an abrupt change in its power position, the major power faces uncertainty and is forced to search for new foreign policy roles. At this point, it is vulnerable to overreaction, such as seeking to prevent the loss of dependent territory through use of military force.

Beyond the status of the imperial/colonial power, consideration must also be given to the territory itself. National independence is often a contentious issue between the imperial/colonial power and the local population. Research has indicated that mediation is less successful when the issues involved are regarded as very important.[39] Military conflict may be more likely when the territory has great intrinsic or relational importance. An imperial/colonial power may be more willing to fight to retain an important dependent territory, and thereby keep the accompanying benefits of that control.

We believe that another influence on the state formation conflicts is the prevailing norms in the international system. In this context, a norm exists when states "usually act in a certain way and are often punished when seen not to be acting in this way."[40] State formation conflicts should be less likely if a norm against such violence (or in support of independence) exists in the international system. Such a norm has developed, and states and their dependent territories may fight over territorial control less under these circumstances.

The norm of peaceful transition to statehood seems to have developed in two different ways. First, imperial/colonial powers came to develop the norm of not resisting with military force the desire of some of their dependent territories to be independent. This can occur after the imperial/colonial power has unsuccessfully tried to resist previous independence efforts. In a broader context, Axelrod argues that states will reemploy strategies that were successful in the past, but discard those that were failures.[41] If an imperial/colonial power failed to stop indigenous groups who sought independence in the past, it might be reluctant to use military force in the future under similar circumstances. This norm against using force and supporting a peaceful transition would be strengthened by the punishment (for example, the military costs in lives and material and the criticism from the international community) resulting from such action. We would expect that the first few times an imperial/colonial power relinquishes sovereignty to a new state, military conflict would be likely. Yet, the greater the number of previous cases of ceding independence a power has, the stronger the norm against military conflict in national independence cases becomes, and the more willing the imperial/colonial power will be to transfer territorial control peacefully.

The second source for the norm against military conflict in state formation cases has its roots immediately following World War II. Article 1 (2) of the United Nations Charter makes reference to the right of self-determination of people, suggesting that imperial/colonial domination is wrong. Various early UN resolutions reflected this same sentiment, and the world community began to accept the idea that imperial/colonial powers should give up their possessions.[42] A major event in the development of a norm of decolonization was the passage of General Assembly Resolution 1514 in 1960. This resolution effectively equates imperial/colonial domination with a violation of human rights and declares that such domination is contrary to the UN Charter. Over time, this resolution and the principles contained in it have been cited again and again, both in subsequent UN resolutions and opinions of the International Court of Justice. The right of self-determination may even have acquired legal standing as a "preemptory norm" of international law.[43] Those who violate this norm have been subject to international condemnation and, in the case of Israel and South Africa, subject to political and economic sanctions.

The achievement of independence by a dependent territory is a special kind of territorial transfer. Although research on the subject is sparse, it seems that conflicts over territory in the state formation process are most likely when the territory is considered important, the imperial/colonial power is declining in its power, and there is no prevailing norm in the international system against such conflict. We fully discuss and test these propositions in chapter 3.

INTERSTATE CONFLICTS

Rather than conflict arising from national independence and the desire of states to hold onto dependent territories, we turn our attention to conflict over homeland territory between established members of the international system. Territorial disputes are often the basis for war as states seek to seize or hold onto land areas through the use of military force. Indeed, one legal scholar contends that the use of coercion is still the principle feature of settling boundary disputes.[44]

Kratochwil, Rohrlich, and Mahajan identify three different types of disputes over sovereignty.[45] A positional dispute derives from the uncertainty over the exact location of boundary lines. A functional boundary dispute involves disagreement over utilization of a transboundary resource; disagreements over the law of the sea and Antarctica are notable examples. They also define the third kind, territorial disputes, as involving the formation of social systems, with concern for molding peoples of similar ethnic and cultural backgrounds into one nation-state.

One might expect that each kind of dispute would have a different likelihood of occurrence and propensity for military conflict. Mandel reports that an ethnic problem, rather than a desire for more resources, has a greater likelihood of producing a border dispute.[46] In contrast, "lateral pressure" models of expansion emphasize that it is the drive for resources and internal growth that produces territorial conflict.[47] An early twentieth century geographer, Thomas Holdich, predicted in 1916 that there would be few border disputes in the eastern, British regions of Africa because the boundary lines were so carefully drawn; this reflects a belief that geographic disputes are largely a product of uncertainty over boundary lines.

If the frequency of certain types of territorial disputes is not clear, even less apparent are the conditions for military conflict in those disputes. Many of the propositions put forward parallel the research in the international conflict literature. For example, Prescott believes that territorial disputes occur following a change in the relative strength of the states involved. Once that change in the power distribution has occurred, the stronger state will be in a position to press its claims.[48] These ideas are consistent with those of scholars who identify a status quo and revisionist power and predict war when the revisionist gains an advantage. Consistent with ambiguous findings of the literature on power distribution and war,[49] others indicate that border disputes are more prevalent when there is an equal distribution of power between the protagonists. Other explanations center on some characteristics of the states involved, such as their level of technology or the stability of their governments. The latter is illustrated by the Argentine invasion of the Falklands and the moves by Indonesian President Sukarno against Malaysia during periods of domestic political unrest in his country.

When analysts have looked at territorial conflict, they have done so in a limited and conventional way. The explanations for whether military conflict has occurred or whether the dispute was resolved peacefully relate to the attributes of the states or pairs of states in the dispute; the relational and intrinsic importance of the territory to the states involved are ignored. In chapter 4, we investigate more closely these concerns.

TERRITORY AND RECURRING CONFLICT

The final point of concern is the problem of recurring conflict between states. Unlike the previous two areas, we look here not to the bases of territorial conflict, but to its future consequences. The cessation of a territorial dispute does not necessarily signal the end of conflict between the states involved. Competing claims over territory have often led to repeated battles between the same pair of states. Erich Weede claims that "the history of war and peace is largely identical with the history of territorial changes as results of war and causes of the next war."[50] Five wars have been fought in the Middle East since 1945 over the question of territorial sovereignty. The creation of the Israeli state was the starting point of the conflict, and subsequent violent adjustments in territorial control have only seemed to generate further hostilities. Nevertheless, the creation of new states and the transfer of territory does not always precipitate future conflict. The Spanish-American War and the resulting acquisition of territory by the United States, for example, ushered in an era of peaceful relations between the United States and Spain.

When do territorial changes signal the end of conflict and when do they only represent the beginning of the struggle? Much like the decision-makers they study, scholars have often taken a very narrow view of military conflict, focusing on only one crisis or war (and the conditions surrounding it) at one particular point in time. Even when a broad historical outlook is adopted, the dispute or war is often regarded as the endpoint, not the beginning of a rivalry.

There have been few efforts to look at the impact of prior conflict on future conflict behavior. Levy and Morgan find that neither great power war nor its severity exercises much impact on subsequent war involvement; in effect, they find no support for the "war-weariness" hypothesis.[51] Singer and Cusack come to a similar conclusion, with the exception that defeated powers delay entry into their next war if the last war was particularly severe.[52] Stoll finds nations only slightly less involved in militarized disputes in the ten year period immediately following a war.[53] In general, it appears that prior war experience is unrelated or, at best, very weakly related to future conflict involvement.

The preceding studies focus on the general conflict behavior of individual states; they reveal little about the likelihood of future conflict between any given *pair* of nations. Studies of conflict diffusion do look at future conflict; states with warring borders are found to have a greater propensity than other states to be involved in the year after their neighbor's war involvement. Yet, such studies do not investigate future war between the same pair of states nor do they consider future conflict in a long time frame.

Rather than explore general propensities for future conflict, we are concerned with whether states engage in lasting enmities with one another. On this subject, the evidence is again limited. Weede reports that if a dyad experiences a territorial change, and if the territory is directly contiguous to both states, these states have an increased likelihood of engaging in military conflict with one another at a later time.[54] Although his concern is exclusively with prior coalition partners in a war, Starr finds that an unequal distribution of spoils (for example, territory) among coalition members increases the likelihood that the partners will end up on opposite sides in a future war.[55] Thus, the perceived legitimacy of the territorial transfer and its geographical location may be significant in affecting future prospects for military conflict.

Several studies identify "enduring rivalries" in which the same pair of states clashes in two or more disputes over a protracted period of time.[56] The primary concern of these studies, however, is to identify the existence of enduring rivalries; questions concerning the causes of the rivalry or the timing of the confrontations generally are not addressed. Yet, the relatively large number of these rivalries indicates that recurring conflict is not uncommon.

Although we may be uncertain as to why conflict between any given dyad of states reoccurs, we should not mistake its consequences. Leng found that states adopt more coercive bargaining strategies in successive disputes with the same enemy, and the result was almost always war by the third confrontation.[57] This highlights the importance of settling initial conflicts, lest they escalate to higher levels of violence. Chapter 5 explores the conditions under which a change in territorial sovereignty leads to recurring military conflict between the parties.

We hope to achieve several theoretical goals in our analyses. First, we evaluate the utility of the realpolitik approach in understanding territorial conflict. We assess its utility by including power politics factors in our models of conflict for each of the three problem areas. In addition, however, we also include factors influencing decisions to use military force not envisioned by the realpolitik approach. These include, for example, international norms and the intrinsic importance of territory. Thus, we hope to determine if the power politics factors are useful in predicting military conflict and then assess their relative utility to the nonpower politics concerns.

Second, in a related concern, we hope to demonstrate that scholars of territorial conflict, and of international relations in general, need to account for the issues and their salience in a dispute to understand fully national decisions to use military force. By looking to the importance of territory and evaluating its influence on decisions for military force in three problem areas, we believe that the willingness of states to use such force can be better understood and scholars will be encouraged to pursue considerations of issue salience in future research.

The next chapter is concerned with patterns of territorial change over the period 1815 to 1980. In that chapter, we present a territorial history of the international system and identify a number of the relevant attributes of changes in territorial sovereignty. Furthermore, we seek to identify patterns in those changes across time and with respect to the behavior of various states. Having set the stage with this description, we devote the next three chapters to the three topics noted above: state-formation conflicts, territorial conflict between states, and recurring conflict. In the concluding chapter, we hope to offer insights on the various issues discussed in this first chapter.

Notes

1. Robert O'Connell, *Of Arms and Men: A History of War, Weapons and Aggression* (New York: Oxford University Press, 1989), 30–31.
2. Harold Sprout and Margaret Sprout, *The Ecological Perspective on Human Affairs* (Princeton: Princeton University Press, 1965).
3. Kenneth Boulding, *Conflict and Defense* (New York: Harper and Row, 1962).

4. Harvey Starr, "Opportunity and Willingness as Ordering Concepts in the Study of War," *International Interactions* 4 (1978):363–387; see also Benjamin Most and Harvey Starr, *Inquiry, Logic, and International Politics* (Columbia: University of South Carolina Press, 1989).
5. Starr, "Opportunity and Willingness":364.
6. Bruce Russett, "A Macroscopic View of International Politics" in *The Analysis of International Politics*, eds. James Rosenau, Vincent Davis, and Maurice East (New York: Free Press, 1972), 109–124.
7. Starr, "Opportunity and Willingness," 370.
8. See Harvey Starr, "Opportunity, Borders, and the Diffusion of International Conflict: An Overview and Some Observations" (Working Paper presented at the Annual Meeting of the American Political Science Association, Chicago, 1987).
9. Istvan Kende, "Twenty-Five Years of Local Wars," *Journal of Peace Research* 2 (1971):5–22.
10. James Wesley, "Frequency of Wars and Geographical Opportunity," *Journal of Conflict Resolution* 6 (1962):387–389.
11. Lewis Richardson, *Statistics of Deadly Quarrels* (Pittsburgh: Boxwood Press, 1960).
12. Consistent with the notion that shared borders increase the likelihood of war is the finding that proximate pairs of states are more likely to fight each other. See David Garnham, "Dyadic International War, 1816–1965: The Role of Power Parity and Geographic Proximity," *Western Political Quarterly* 27 (1976):97–120.
13. Harvey Starr and Benjamin Most, "The Substance and Study of Borders in International Relations Research," *International Studies Quarterly* 20 (1976):581–620, and Harvey Starr and Benjamin Most, "A Return Journey: Richardson, Frontiers, and Wars in the 1946–65 Era," *Journal of Conflict Resolution* 22 (1978):441–467.
14. Harvey Starr and Benjamin Most, "Contagion and Border Effects on Contemporary African Conflict," *Comparative Political Studies* 16 (1983):92–117.
15. Manus Midlarsky, *On War* (New York: Free Press, 1975).
16. Differing views on the role of uncertainty and the outbreak of war are at the heart of the debate on polarity and war as evidenced in Karl Deutsch and J. David Singer, "Multipolar Power Systems and International Stability," *World Politics* 16 (1964):390–406 and Kenneth Waltz, "The Stability of a Bipolar World," *Daedalus* 93 (1964):881–909; for further discussion of uncertainty and war, see Bruce Bueno de Mesquita, *The War Trap* (New Haven: Yale University Press, 1981).
17. Paul F. Diehl, "Contiguity and Military Escalation in Major Power Rivalries, 1816–1980," *Journal of Politics* 47 (1985):1203–1211.
18. For a review of literature on diffusion, see Benjamin Most, Harvey Starr, and Randolph Siverson, "The Logic and Study of the Diffusion of International War" in *The Handbook of War Studies*, ed. Manus Midlarsky (Boston: Unwin Hyman, 1989):111–139.
19. Marc Ross and Elizabeth Homer, "Galton's Problem in Cross-National Research," *World Politics* 29 (1976):1–28.

20. Benjamin Most and Harvey Starr, "Diffusion, Reinforcement, Geopolitics, and the Spread of War," *American Political Science Review* 74 (1980):932–946; Starr and Most, "Contagion and Border Effects"; Harvey Starr and Benjamin Most, "The Forms and Processes of War Diffusion: Research Update on Contagion in African Conflict," *Comparative Political Studies* 18 (1985):206–227.
21. In the context of conflict studies, addiction refers to the propensity for one state to have repeated experiences with war over time. Contagion refers to the spread of conflict from one state to another. For an example of the disease analogy, see Norman Alcock, *The War Disease* (Oakville, Ont.: CPRI Press, 1972).
22. William Davis, George Duncan, and Randolph Siverson, "The Dynamics of Warfare," *American Journal of Political Science* 22 (1978):772–792.
23. Stuart Bremer, "The Contagiousness of Coercion: The Spread of Serious International Disputes, 1900–1976," *International Interactions* 9 (1982):29–55.
24. Jan Faber, Henk Houweling, and Jan Siccama, "Diffusion of War: Some Theoretical Considerations and Empirical Evidence," *Journal of Peace Research* 21 (1984):277–288.
25. Henk Houweling and Jan Siccama, "The Epidemiology of War, 1960–1980," *Journal of Conflict Resolution* 29 (1985):641–663.
26. Benjamin Most, Philip Schrodt, Randolph Siverson, and Harvey Starr, "Border and Alliance Effects in the Diffusion of Major Power Conflict, 1815–1865" in *Prisoners of War?: Nation-States in the Modern Era*, eds. Charles Gochman and Alan Sabrosky C Lexington, Mass.: Lexington Books, 1990), 209–230. See also Randolph Siverson and Harvey Starr, "Opportunity, Willingness, and the Diffusion of War, 1816–1965," *American Political Science Review* 84 (1990):47–68.
27. See Nicholas Spykman *The Geography of the Peace* (New York: Harcourt Brace, 1944) and Halford Mackinder, *Democratic Ideals and Reality* (New York: Henry Holt, 1919).
28. James Lee Ray, *Global Politics*, 3rd ed. (Boston: Houghton–Mifflin, 1987), 478.
29. See Howard Koch, Robert North, and Dina Zinnes, "Some Theoretical Notes on Geography and International Conflict," *Journal of Conflict Resolution* 4 (1960):4–14.
30. V.I. Lenin, *Imperialism: The Highest Stage of Capitalism* (New York: International Publishers, 1939).
31. This is similar to the notion of *lateral pressure* in Nazli Choucri and Robert North, *Nations in Conflict* (San Francisco: W. H. Freeman, 1975). In their analyses, lateral pressure is operationally defined as an increase in territory.
32. Norbert Elias, *Power and Civility* (New York: Pantheon, 1952).
33. Diehl, "Contiguity and Military Escalation." It might be noted, however, that geography may not be as important a determinant in major power interventions. See Frederic Pearson, "Geographic Proximity and Foreign Military Intervention," *Journal of Conflict Resolution* 18 (1974):432–460.

34. Boulding, *Conflict and Defense*. Although Boulding is most often cited for elucidating the idea of "the further, the weaker," a similar point is made almost 50 years earlier by Thomas Holdich, *Political Frontiers and Boundary Making* (London: Macmillan, 1916), 31 and 42. Holdich emphasizes not the problems associated with conducting military missions far from a home base, but the increasing difficulty of sustaining control of territories far away from the locus of power.
35. See Ivo Duchacek, *The Territorial Dimension of Politics: Within, Among, and Across Nations* (Boulder: Westview Press, 1986), 9–10.
36. This argument is made in William Thompson and Gary Zuk, "World Power and the Strategic Trap of Territorial Commitments," *International Studies Quarterly* 30 (1986):249–267. A similar point is made in Paul Kennedy, *The Rise and Fall of the Great Powers* (New York: Random House, 1987).
37. See George Modelski, "The Long Cycle of Global Politics and the Nation-State," *Comparative Studies in Society and History* 20 (1978):214–235.
38. Charles Doran and Wes Parsons, "War and the Cycle of Relative Power," *American Political Science Review* 74 (1980):947–965.
39. J. Bercovitch, "Third Parties in Conflict Management: The Structure and Conditions of Effective Mediation in International Relations," *International Journal* 40 (1965):736–752.
40. Robert Axelrod, "An Evolutionary Approach to Norms," *American Political Science Review* 80 (1986):1095–1111.
41. Ibid.
42. See Harold Jacobson, "The United Nations and Colonialism," *International Organization* 16 (1962):37–56.
43. Malcolm Shaw, *Title to Territory in Africa* (Oxford: Clarendon Press, 1986).
44. Surya Sharma, *International Boundary Disputes and International Law* (Bombay: Tripathi, 1976), 2.
45. Friedrich Kratochwil, Paul Rohrlich, and Harpreet Mahajan, *Peace and Disputed Sovereignty: Reflections on Conflict Over Territory* (Lanham, Maryland: University Press of America, 1985), 18–19.
46. Robert Mandel, "Roots of Modern Interstate Border Disputes," *Journal of Conflict Resolution* 24 (1980):450.
47. Choucri and North, *Nations in Conflict*.
48. J.R.V. Prescott, *The Geography of Frontiers and Boundaries* (Chicago: Aldine Publishing, 1965), 114.
49. For a summary of this literature, see Randolph Siverson and Michael Sullivan, "The Distribution of Power and the Onset of War," *Journal of Conflict Resolution* 27 (1983):473–494.
50. Erich Weede, "Nation-Environment Relations as Determinants of Hostilities Among Nations," *Peace Science Society (International) Papers* 20 (1973):87.
51. Jack Levy and T. Clifton Morgan, "The War Weariness Hypothesis: An Empirical Test," *American Journal of Political Science* 30 (1986):26–50.
52. J. David Singer and Thomas Cusack, "Periodicity, Inexorability, and Steermanship in International War" in *From National Development to*

Global Community: Essays in Honor of Karl Deutsch, eds. Richard Merritt and Bruce Russett (London: Allen and Unwin, 1981), 404–422.
53. Richard Stoll, "From Fire to Frying Pan: The Impact of Major Power War Involvement on Major Power Dispute Involvement, 1816–1975," *Conflict Management and Peace Science* 7 (1984):71–82.
54. Erich Weede, "World Order in the Fifties and Sixties: Dependence, Deterrence, and Limited Peace," *Peace Science Society (International) Papers* 24 (1975):49–80 and Weede, "Nation-Environment Relations."
55. Harvey Starr, *Coalitions and Future War: A Dyadic Study of Cooperation and Conflict* (Sage Professional Papers in International Studies, V. 3. Beverly Hills, Calif.: Sage Publications 1975).
56. Frank Wayman, "War and Power Transitions During Enduring Rivalries" (Paper presented at the Institute for the Study of Conflict Theory and International Conflict, Champaign–Urbana, 1982); Charles Gochman and Zeev Maoz, "Militarized Interstate Disputes, 1816–1976: Procedures, Patterns, and Insights," *Journal of Conflict Resolution* 28 (1984):585–616; Paul Diehl, "Arms Races to War: Testing Some Empirical Linkages," *Sociological Quarterly* 26 (1985):331–349.
57. Russell Leng, "When Will They Ever Learn: Coercive Bargaining in Recurrent Crises," *Journal of Conflict Resolution* 27 (1983):379–419.

CHAPTER 2

A Territorial History of the International System

The two elements that form the focus of this book, territory and military conflict, are also the central components in the popular definition of the nation-state. The usual definition of a nation-state includes *military* control over a defined *territory*. The growth and change of what we commonly call the inter*national* system, is from our point of view, the development of the inter*state* system. Thus, it is when states lose control over territory or gain control over new territory that the physical characteristics of the international system change. The history of the international system is by definition then the relationship between territory and states and how these relationships change over time. Many of these changes have involved serious military conflict but, as we note below, a majority have not. Some have involved the formation of new states, while others constituted an exchange of territory between existing states. In this chapter, we chart the territorial evolution of the international system from the post-Napoleonic Wars to the present.

The history of the international system has yet to be written from the point of view of the rise and development of a quasi-organized system of relationships between entities called nation-states. Various aspects of this process have received extensive attention. The concept of a *sovereign* state is, in part, a legal one. The development, through treaties and custom, of the legal existence of a state has been treated at length by scholars of international law.

The rise and fall of colonial and imperial empires, which dramatically changes the composition of the international system, has been the focus of historians' attention. This research either tends to be historical case studies (for example, of the British Empire) or the classic grand theories of imperialism, notably those of the Marxist tradition such as Lenin, or other approaches such as that of Schumpeter.[1] Historians have also looked at the major power states, analyzing territorial issues and changes in the context of major power war. Finally, the "formal" or "political" organization of the international system has been studied by international organization scholars. The recent fascination with the concept of an "international regime"[2] reflects a less formal, less state-based concern with the organization of the system.

Although the concept of an international system has been part of the intellectual baggage of international relations scholars for at least several decades, it has not surfaced as a legitimate object of study in its own right. At first glance, studies on the world system might be seen as addressing this issue, but a closer look reveals that this is not the case. At best, the structure of the world system—whatever this is taken to mean in any given study—is the independent variable (to use statistical terminology), but is rarely the dependent variable. The remainder of this chapter describes the territorial evolution of the international system from 1816 to 1980. We first describe the metamorphosis of the system from a basically European one around 1816 to a global one in 1980. We then examine how these changes were effected, and conclude by identifying the important actors that brought about these changes.

The Evolution of the Interstate System

Before describing the rise and transformation of the international system, it is necessary to discuss briefly our unit of analysis, the nation-state. The work of J. David Singer and the Correlates of War (COW) Project is one of the few enterprises in the social sciences that has seriously grappled with a definition of the interstate system for the nineteenth and twentieth centuries. A major problem is how to evaluate which territories are part of the system (that is, nation-states) and which are outside of that realm. The COW Project solution for the twentieth century is to use the League of Nations and the United Nations as international "legitimizers" in defining what political units are considered states (a few exceptions are made in the case of states not belonging to these bodies, such as Switzerland and the Koreas). For the nineteenth century, they use the United Kingdom and France as international legitimizers, while excluding political units with a population of less than 500,000. These operational definitions of a state are eminently political ones. Economic importance or size is irrelevant as is any social-cultural distinction. The territorial history that we outline here is thus a history of states.[3]

In our analysis of the growth of the international system we use three measures of its size. One is the number of new states that enter the system at any given time.[4] The other two are the population and geographic area encompassed by the international system.[5] The number of states added to the system in any five-year period is only moderately correlated with the area ($r=.58$) and population ($r=.50$) added. Population and area are clearly related, although the correlation is still modest ($r=.44$).[6] One should recognize, however, that unlike area, population in the international system is capable of drawing much of its increase from its own base; there are physical limits to the area that can be encompassed in the system whereas population may not have so well-defined a limit. Thus, one might expect the same area to include larger populations over time. During some periods, a few changes have dramatic effects on the area and population of the international system, such as the entry of India in 1947.

From our point of view, the most important of the growth indicators is the number of states on the international scene. Figure 2.1 reveals that the international system grows from a modest size of 23 states in 1816 to almost 160 states in 1980. Through the addition of Latin American and European states, the international system grows at about the rate of one state every year during the first part of the nineteenth century. By this time, several large empires are already well established, including those of the Spanish, Portuguese, English, Ottoman, and Austro-Hungarian. The number of states in the international system declines slightly around 1860 as a result of the Italian and German unifications. Following that drop, however, the system resumes the growth rate prevalent in the earlier part of the century.

Both World Wars represent ruptures and changes in the international system. One result is that dramatic numbers of new states are added to the system. The weakening of the defeated adversary often ends in the formation of new states from the territory it formerly controlled. Centuries before, this territory would have been incorporated into the winning states' territory, but this practice has virtually disappeared by the twentieth century. A major exception is the Soviet Union's incorporation of part of eastern Poland after the Second World War. Exceptions to the standard against incorporating the defeated powers' territory seem to occur when the area is contiguous to the victorious state(s).

Figure 2.1 Entries into the International System

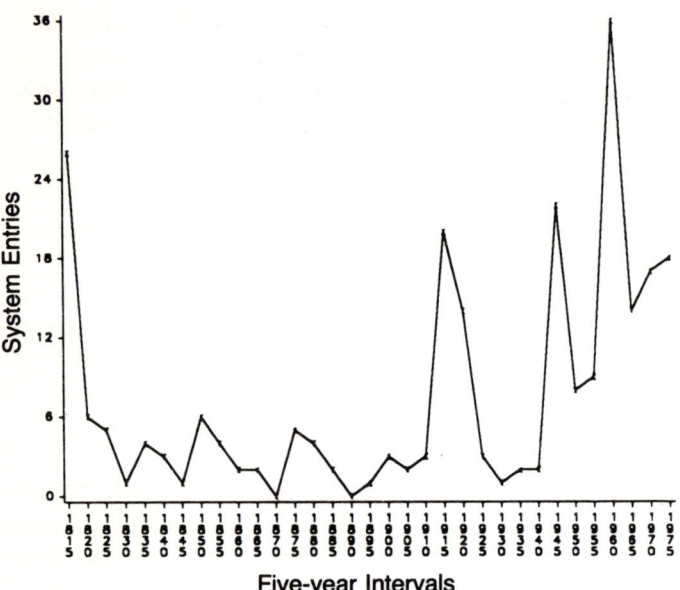

Partially as a result of World War II, but somewhat delayed in time, is the explosion of new states starting in the 1950s and continuing until the late 1970s. Thus, from the point of view of the international system, World War II constitutes a watershed; membership in the system more than doubles from 1945 to 1980. Since 1980, however, only seven new states have been admitted to the United Nations. At present, new territories are no longer being settled and most of the world from the Arctic to the Antarctic Circles is divided into nation-states. Protectorates, mandated territories, and colonies have declined substantially. If the international system is to add additional states, many would have to come from the territories of existing states. Unless a major war were to break out, it is difficult to imagine large numbers of new states entering the system.[7]

Just as there have been differences across time in the international system, so too has the international system grown unevenly across space. Table 2.1 shows the changes in the regional distribution of states from 1816 to 1980. In 1816, only the United States and the Ottoman Empire keep the international system from being completely Eurocentric. There are relatively few additions in Europe during the nineteenth century except for the period around 1860. The dramatic change on this continent occurred after World War I with the breakup of the Ottoman and Austro-Hungarian Empires. After these events, the European subsystem is in its basic outlines formed. The only subsequent major change is the division of Germany after World War II.

Table 2.1 Regional Distribution of States, 1816 to 1980

Region	1816	1870	1920	1945	1980
Americas	1	13	22	22	31
Europe	21	17	27	26	29
Africa	0	0	3	3	45
Middle East	1	3	3	7	21
Asia	0	2	7	8	29
Total	23	35	62	66	155

In the Western Hemisphere, changes came in three waves. Most of the large countries of South America are members of the international system by 1860. Central American states join the system at the turn of the century. A third wave occurs when a small number of colonies, especially in the Caribbean, become independent in the post-World War II era of decolonization. Middle East states emerge only after World Wars I and II. Asian entries into the system come early for the major powers, Japan and China, and later for smaller states in the decolonization movement of the 1950s and 1960s. As the scene of major power activities, Asian and African territories must await the breakup of the European empires before gaining independence.

The growth in the population and territorial area of the international system is considerably more uneven. In some respects, increases in the area and population of the international system are a better indicator of the political significance of the changes because larger and more populous states are generally more powerful ones. Given the large differences in population and territory among states, the entry of a state such as India is the equivalent to the entry of 20 to 30 small states. Figures 2.2 and 2.3 show the addition of population and area to the system since 1816.

Although the international system grows in the nineteenth century with a slow, but steady, addition of states, the population and area encompassed by the system show few dramatic changes until the twentieth century. This reflects that the international system only grew slowly in this period and that prior to decolonization there were still whole continents and large numbers of people that were not part of the system. The population gains by the system are not only the result of many new states in the system, but also the dramatic population growth in those territories prior to entering the system. The analysis of population and area growth confirm what was apparent in the analysis of states: most of the growth in the international system occurs in the twentieth century, following the World Wars.

Until now, we have discussed the growth of the international system, but states can leave, as well as enter, the system. Overall, such instances of the former are comparatively rare ($N=18$). The only notable period for exits from the international system occurs during the time of German and Italian unification. Several states disappear briefly or permanently during and after World War II, with Lithuania being a notable example. Because most states do not disappear voluntarily, with an exception or two such as the United Arab Republic (the former union of Egypt and Syria), most disappearances are the results of wars or military threats (for example, the *Anschluss*).

Territorial Changes in the International System

In the previous section, we charted the growth of the international system with particular reference to the number of actors that joined

Figure 2.2 Population Added to the System

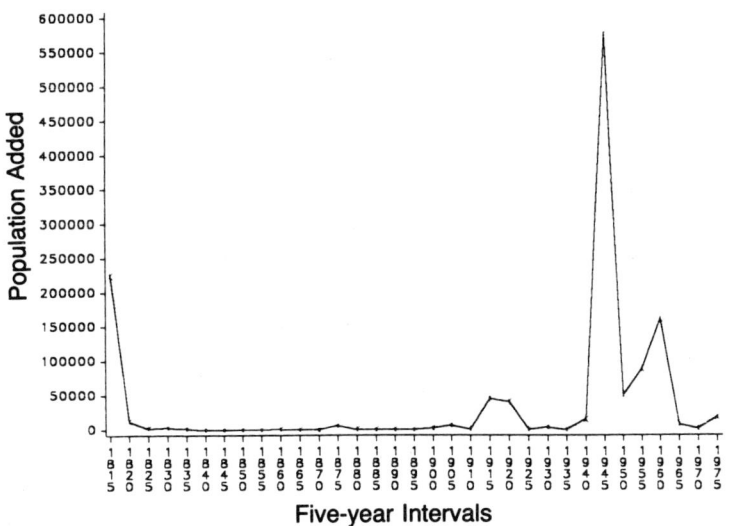

Figure 2.3 Area Added to the System

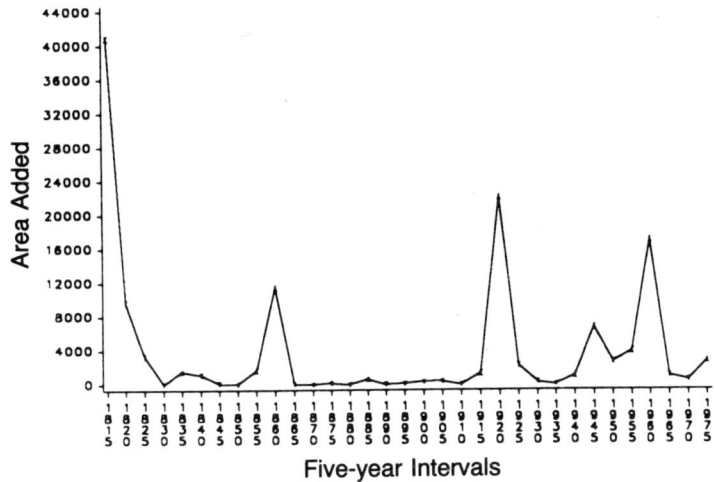

the system. Yet, growth is only one aspect of the history of the international system and its changes. There have been numerous territorial changes that have not necessarily resulted in the addition of new states to the international system. Therefore, we shift our attention to the transfer of territorial control in the international system; many of these changes precipitated military conflict or resulted from it.

For the purposes of this book, a territorial change is said to occur when a political entity gains or loses any portion of a territorial unit. The term *political entity* is used to describe states and territory-based nonstates or quasi-states (for example, colonies, protectorates, and mandate territories). Not all territorial changes are included in our analyses. First, only those changes involving at least one state are included. Thus, such changes as the secession of the United States of Central America from Mexico are not included because neither political entity was a member of the international system at the time of the change. This restriction has practical as well as theoretical reasons. We are unable to identify the seemingly thousands of territorial changes that take place between nonstates; the most common example would be the ever-shifting informal boundaries between tribal or nomadic groups. More important, however, we are interested in international conflict and not civil warfare between quasi-organized entities. We wish to keep our attention exclusively on territorial conflict involving the major actors in international relations—nation-states.

Our analysis also excludes territorial changes that occurred north of the Arctic Circle and south of the Antarctic Circle. This is done because of the overlapping claims in the area, the lack of effective occupation, and the failure of most major powers to recognize these claims. A related problem occurs when colonial powers merely drew lines on a map, especially in Africa, in order to decide which territories would belong to which states. Such agreements are not treated as territorial changes in most cases unless there was effective occupation.

Despite these limitations, 770 cases of territorial change satisfy the criteria outlined here, including cases of dependent territories becoming independent states.[8] Pinpointing the exact date of the changes is obvious in most cases, but there was some difficulty in some instances. Some changes, for example, occurred during wartime and were confirmed later by provisions of a peace treaty.

The rule of thumb was to use the date of the treaty for the time that the territorial change was considered to have taken place. If no treaty was involved in the change, then the date of transfer was when the action to take the territory ceased, when a plebiscite occurred, or when an act of annexation took place. In other cases, the acquisition of dependent territory occurred in piecemeal fashion (for example, the gradual encroachment of Portugal into Angola). The results of such incremental acquisitions are considered as one incidence of territorial change. If the territory was declared a colony on a particular date, then that date was entered as the time of acquisition of the entire territory.

Figure 2.4 Nonindependence Changes in the System

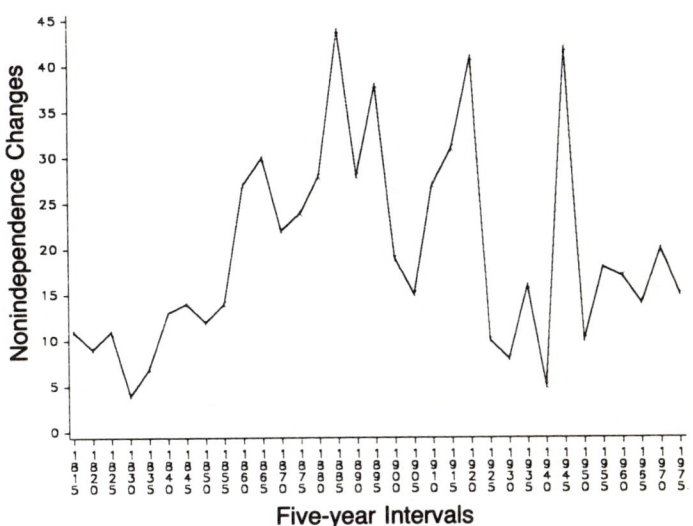

CHANGES IN THE INTERNATIONAL SYSTEM

Figure 2.4 charts the total number of territorial changes, excluding those involving national independence, for the period from 1816 to 1980. In effect, this indicates how the configuration, not the size (that is, number of members), of the international system has changed.

It is clear that territorial changes involving states occur at a rate of about four or five per year. There appears, however, to be no secular trend over the whole period. Nevertheless, there are several peaks that roughly correspond to important changes in the structure of the international system. The first peak occurs at the time of German and Italian unifications in the mid-nineteenth century. Beyond the other territorial changes occurring around this time, Germany and Italy slowly acquired provinces and territories as they forged the modern states that we know today. Two other peaks center around World Wars I and II. Recall that Choucri and North saw territorial expansion as an important measure of the process leading up to World War I.[9] These conflicts precipitated numerous territorial transfers as states permanently conquered or acquired land during the course of the war. The Soviet acquisition of the Sakhalin Islands is a prominent example. In addition, many territorial transfers resulted from peace treaties at the conclusion of those wars. Territory was transferred as compensation for war debts as well as a punitive measure against the defeated power. After the First World War in particular, some colonial territory was taken from the losing powers and given to others under the League of Nations mandate system; Palestine has become the most famous example of this type of exchange.

Finally, two peaks represent the rise and the decline of the colonial system. One peak is in the 1880s and 1890s when the second wave of colonial acquisitions among European powers took place. A primary target of those acquisitions was the African subcontinent. The other peak, some 80 years later in the 1960s, is the time when many of those same territories gained their independence as the number of states in the international system grew tremendously in this period of decolonization.

It is conceivable that the patterns noted in Figure 2.4 are deceiving given that the frequency of territorial changes may be a function of the number of states in the international system. Gochman and Maoz found that the frequency of militarized disputes, for example, was strongly related to the size of the international system.[10] The larger the number of states (and resultantly contiguous states), the more "opportunity" for territorial disputes and change. To test this proposition, we standardized the number of territorial changes occurring in the five-year periods, dividing them by the number of states in the international system at the time. In this way, we look at the number of territorial changes in recognition of the size of the international system.

Generally, the patterns are similar to those of the unstandardized results in Figure 2.4. The same five peaks are evident, but those in the post-World War II era look less dramatic when the number of states is considered. Nevertheless, it appears that the relative frequency of territorial change is less sensitive to growth in the international system than are militarized disputes. It should be recognized, however, that territorial changes lead to the creation of new states and thereby increase the size of the international system. Therefore, it is not surprising that when one controls for system size, there is no dramatic change in the pattern of territorial changes.

Many of the changes noted above involved the transfer of a dependent territory which was not formally part of the international system. Perhaps more illuminating is an analysis of the exchange of territory within the system (that is, the transfer of homeland territory between states). Figure 2.5[11] identifies the patterns of those 209 "interstate" changes since 1816; the 160 cases that involve states on both sides of the exchange are the subjects of investigation in chapter 4. An example of this kind of exchange is the absorption of part of Poland by the Soviet Union at the conclusion of World War II.

In the nineteenth century, transfer of homeland territory was relatively rare in comparison with transfers involving dependent territory. Once unsettled territory diminished, states apparently had to acquire territory of other states in order to expand. The periods preceding the World Wars were times of intense activity in homeland transfers; in addition to armaments competition, these times evidently involved other forms of potentially conflictive international interactions.

Other kinds of changes include imperial/colonial transfers, when land held as dependent territory by one side becomes dependent territory of the gaining side. An example of this is the British acquisition of Togoland from Germany in 1899. There were 75 changes of this type from 1816 to 1980. Another kind is mixed transfer, when land held as dependent territory by the yielding side becomes nondependent territory of the acquiring side *or* when nondependent territory of the yielding side becomes dependent territory of the gaining side. An example of this is the minor border adjustment in 1903 between the United States and Canada, completed with British approval. These numbered 398 cases over the period under study.

Figure 2.5 Interstate Changes in the System

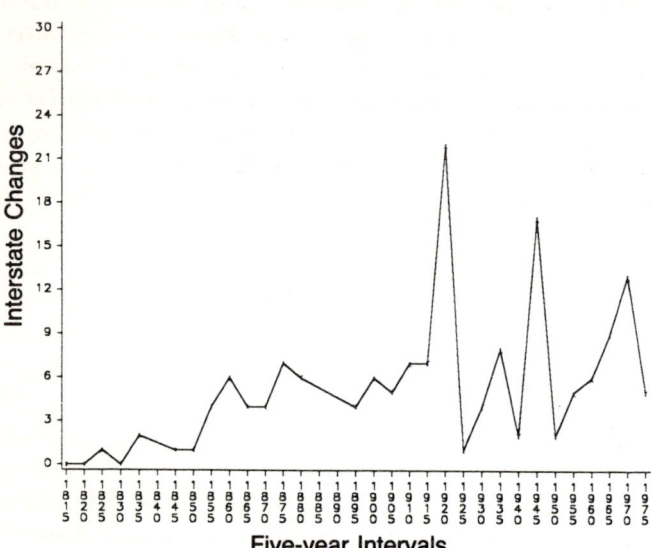

A fourth category, numbering 88, is a residual category, "Other," which consists of all other instances of territorial change not satisfying the criteria for the three previous categories. These include many cases of national independence and a few instances in which the acquiring or yielding side is not a state. An example is the independence of Peru from Spain in 1821.

As these numbers indicate, the number of changes involving dependent territory is substantial, even though our records date back to only 1816, well after the onset of colonialism. Furthermore, approximately 48 percent of territorial transfers include nonstate entities. This suggests that despite the dominance of the nation-state after the Congress of Vienna, other political entities play an important role in international intercourse that we normally think of as reserved to states.

Another way to gauge territorial changes over time is to assess their significance in terms of the area and population affected. Large numbers of changes in a given period could entail only minor border adjustments affecting few people. However, the frequency of minuscule territorial transfers is low; most territorial changes involve a large amount of land and a significant number of people are affected by those changes. The median amount of land transferred is 12,715 square kilometers and the median number of people affected is 250,000. Figure 2.6 traces the area affected by territorial changes over time, in the same way the sheer number of changes was noted above.[12] Because of restricted data availability it would be misleading to present a graph of the population changes; nevertheless, an analysis of the available cases does reveal some patterns.

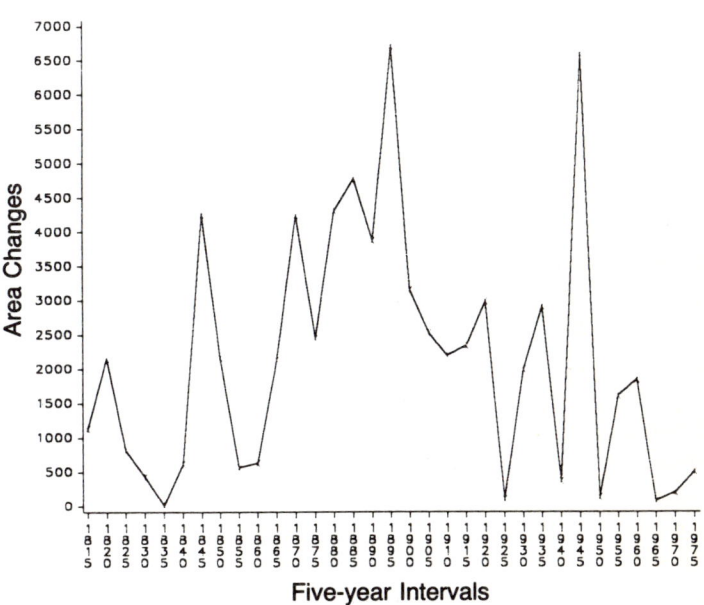

Figure 2.6 Area Changes in the System

The patterns for area and population are quite similar to those for the number of changes. The only exceptions are the tremendous land areas affected by the termination of the two World Wars, and the great number of people affected by territorial changes in the post-1945 era. The latter might be explained by the overall growth in world population, especially after 1945. The peaks remain the same, but they are more pronounced at those times. Indeed, area and population affected are strongly correlated to the frequency of territorial changes ($r=.63$ and $r=.57$ for area and population respectively). The major exception with respect to area is that the peak surrounding World War I is less pronounced, suggesting that although territorial control changed hands frequently, the areas in question were not especially extensive. At the macro level, the number of territorial changes is an indicator of the intrinsic value of the territory exchanged in that period.

Table 2.2 Regional Distribution of Territorial Changes

Asia	Europe	Africa	Americas	Middle East
187	183	190	90	120

If the frequency of territorial changes is not constant over time, neither are the changes evenly distributed across space. We first direct our attention to territorial changes distributed across five regions of the world: Asia, Europe, Africa, the Middle East, and the Americas; Table 2.2 provides these figures. The number of territorial changes is approximately the same in Asia, Europe, and Africa. Africa has a large number of territorial transfers despite the agreement among imperial/colonial powers to carve up Africa among themselves rather than to compete for claims; the Berlin Conference formalized this agreement. Following decolonization, African leaders agreed to respect those boundaries even though they created ethnic and tribal animosities. Yet, because Africa was mainly a collection of dependent territories, a large number of territorial changes took place as various nations gained their independence.

Europe was the centerpiece of the international system for most of the period after the Napoleonic Wars. Because it was fully charted before the period of study and most of the major states were located there, it is perhaps not surprising that territorial change activity was common in that region. The frequency of territorial change in Asia is less apparent at first glance. Yet, that region was a focal point for colonial expansion and competition and many of those territories would later gain their independence with the resulting new states battling each other over disputed territory. The India–Pakistan rivalry is perhaps the most recurrent and intense example of the latter point.

The Middle East and the Americas have relatively fewer territorial transfers than the other regions. The Middle East involves a much smaller land area than the other regions, which may contribute to less frequent changes. Furthermore, more of the changes in this region are of a recent vintage as the colonial system in this region proved to be quite stable compared to the volatile post-World War II period. The dominance of the Western Hemisphere by the United States, the area's relative isolation from Europe, its early colonization, and its comparatively small population may have contributed to the relatively low number of changes there.

In summary, territorial changes in the nineteenth and twentieth century are clustered around major historical events, especially the two World Wars. Beyond shear numbers of territorial changes, the significance of those changes as measured by the size of the area exchanged and the population affected by the change are also coterminous with those events. The typical territorial exchange is hardly insignificant though; several thousand square kilometers populated by a couple of hundred thousand people is the norm (although there is considerable variation in both dimensions). In terms of the kind of land involved (colonial vs. home territory), there is as great a diversity as there is with the geographic region in which the exchange took place, although fewer exchanges occurred in the Middle East and the Western Hemisphere. With these patterns in mind, we shift our analysis to the actors involved in changing the international system.

WHICH STATES HAVE CHANGED THE INTERNATIONAL SYSTEM?

We have looked at the changes that the international system has gone through. The next logical question is: Which states have changed the system? Table 2.3 lists those states that have been involved in at least ten territorial changes. The ten states most involved in territorial changes are hardly surprising. Generally, these are the primary world and imperial/colonial powers over the 165 year period. The United Kingdom and France, with the most numerous and far-flung possessions, easily top the list. Those states with imperial/colonial interests dating before 1816 tended to suffer a net loss in population and area as their imperial/colonial empires were dismantled. There is a consistent shift of territory and population away from a small set of states. Those states on this list which experience a net gain in territory and population are those which gain their independence or unify their nations through territorial acquisition. In the nineteenth century, Germany becomes a modern state and a prominent continental power. One hundred years later, India gains its independence, with its large population and land area. Later, India acquires Goa and further adds to its territorial control. Similar to the relationship noted above, frequency of national involvement in territorial changes is strongly related to the total area and population affected ($r=.93$ and $r=.80$ for area and population respectively).

Except for Spain (which is included in the territorial change list), the top ten states most involved in territorial changes are the same as those most involved in militarized disputes.[13] One explanation for this convergence is that major powers are more likely to participate in all forms of international intercourse, as international trade figures indicate. Thus, there may be no intimate connection between territorial changes and militarized disputes. Yet it may also be that territorial changes accompany interstate disputes with a strong connection between the two phenomena. The remaining part of this book is directed at assessing the existence and extent of the relationship between territorial changes and military conflict in various contexts.

The secular trend with variations is that the early nineteenth and late twentieth century represent periods of reduced major power participation in territorial changes, as noted in Figure 2.7. The period from 1850 to 1914 is the heyday of major power territorial activity; major powers are involved in 73 percent of changes in this period relative to the average of 56 percent in other periods. Overall, the importance of the major powers is great. Representing no more than nine states in any given year, they are involved in more than half of the changes in the international system. If Portugal, Spain, and the Netherlands, which by 1815 are no longer major powers (but once were), are included, the percentage would be even larger. The argument that the characteristics of the international system are the result of major power behavior receives support from this analysis. Nevertheless, we believe it appropriate to note one caveat. There has been a precipitous decline in major power involvement over the last 25 years. The rapid decline in imperial/colonial holdings means that major powers may now only be involved in territorial changes over their home territories. Given the stability of those borders and the absence of major power war, that trend may be likely to continue.

Figure 2.7 Percentage of Major Power Changes

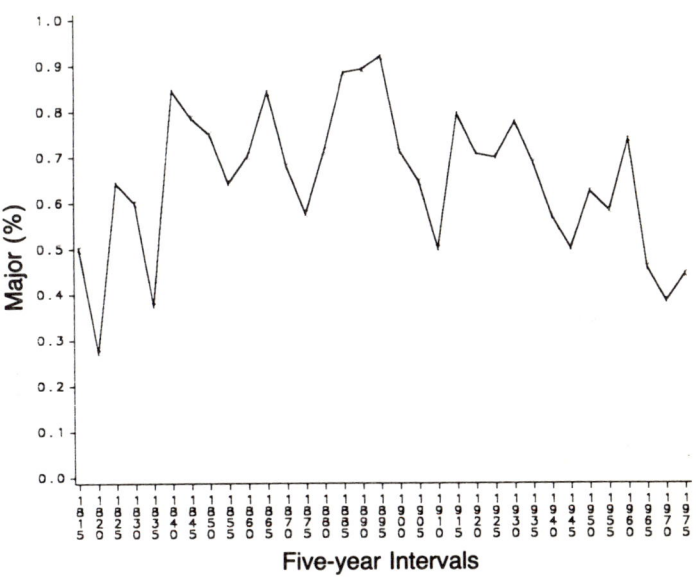

HOW THE SYSTEM HAS CHANGED

In studies of international conflict, it is important to assess whether territorial changes involved military force. Thus, we

Table 2.3 Nations with Greatest Involvement in Territorial Changes, 1816 to 1980

Nation	Frequency			Military Conflict		Area (in hundred thousands)	
	Total	Gain	Loss	N	%	Gain	Loss
United Kingdom	226	125	101	26	11.5	147	384
France	114	69	45	29	25.4	109	126
Germany[a]	81	48	33	20	24.7	25	42
U.S.S.R.[b]	64	22	42	35	54.6	61	45
Turkey[c]	53	12	41	28	52.8	11	44
Italy	47	30	17	22	46.8	32	38
United States	40	26	14	6	15.0	55	10
Spain	31	7	24	9	29.0	4	122
China	25	8	17	11	44.0	25	61
Japan	25	16	9	11	44.0	37	22
Portugal	23	10	13	3	13.0	9	104
Netherlands	20	9	11	5	25.0	5	22
Belgium	19	10	9	2	10.5	1	24
India	18	10	8	4	22.2	29	0.9
Czechoslovakia	15	7	8	5	33.3	4	2
Egypt	15	11	4	12	80.0	64	15
Pakistan	14	8	6	4	28.6	9	3
Yugoslavia	14	11	3	8	57.1	2	0.1
Poland	14	10	4	6	28.6	10	19
Morocco	13	8	4	1	7.7	7	9
Brazil	12	10	2	2	16.7	92	3
Greece	11	9	2	6	54.5	1	.002
Israel	11	6	7	7	63.6	4	0.5

[a] Includes Prussia from 1816 through Germany in 1945.
[b] Includes Russia from 1816 through the U.S.S.R in 1980.
[c] Includes Ottoman Empire from 1816 through Turkey in 1980.

identified whether military conflict was involved in the territorial changes in our study. Military conflict is defined as at least one military encounter between organized forces of the gaining and losing sides.

Because a territorial dispute is primarily zero-sum (usually only one entity can control a piece of land[14]), it may appear surprising that the vast majority of all territorial changes over the last 165 years have been completed peacefully. Nevertheless, many territorial transfers occur by mutual agreement of the parties. The Berlin Conference is an example of a multilateral agreement to peacefully divide territory instead of resorting to armed competition. Furthermore, we must remember that many nations acquired their independence without violence as the mother country eased the transition from colony to independent state.

Figure 2.8 Percentage of Military Conflict Changes

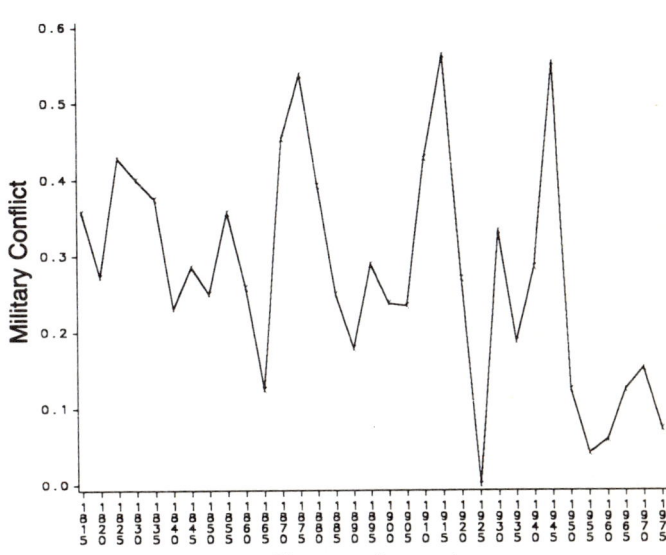

We have discussed the kinds of changes that the international system has undergone, but we are interested in the characteristics of changes that involved military conflict. Do periods of important change—measured by the population and area of the territories transferred—correspond to periods of violent change? Correlations for our five-year time blocks[15] indicate there is little relationship between the aggregate, intrinsic importance of the territory exchanged and the propensity for violence in the five-year period; the correlation coefficients between violence and the intrinsic importance of the territory are .003 and .15 for area and population respectively. The correlation between the number of territorial changes and the percentage that involved military conflict in any five-year period was no more impressive ($r=.12$).

Figure 2.8 charts the percentage of changes involving military conflict over time. If World War II is a watershed in terms of the number of states in the international system, it also constitutes a pivotal point in terms of how the changes were effected. The percentage of changes involving violence oscillates around 33 percent before World War II, yet drops to around 16 percent after 1945. This is not to say that states no longer fight over territorial issues; rather, the use of military force rarely results in the successful exchange of territorial control. As Iraq's attempt to seize territory from Iran in 1979 subsequently demonstrated, it has become much more difficult to acquire new (or in the case of the Falklands War, reacquire old) territory through the vehicle of military force. After eight years of bitter fighting, the Iran–Iraq border now seems likely to be minimally affected by the war.

Table 2.3 shows that there are some startling differences in the frequency of conflict by nation-state. Not only is the Soviet Union among the most involved in territorial changes, but almost half of those changes involved military conflict. Although Russian expansion is often cited, the Soviet Union (and its predecessor Tsarist Russia) lost territory twice as many times as it gained new land. The frequency of military conflict combined with the number of times that territory was lost gives some insight into the Soviet preoccupation with its security and territorial defenses. Noticeably high on the military conflict dimension are Egypt and Israel, who have fought several wars over disputed territory. Being the battle grounds of major powers has also led some states to be involved in a disproportionate frequency of military conflict; Yugoslavia and Turkey (and its predecessor the Ottoman Empire) are most evident.

In addition to whether the change involved military conflict, we also assessed the *process* by which the change took place. We divided the possible procedures for change into seven categories:

1. *Conquest*: When the primary agent of change is armed force, and the change is not formally ratified by treaty. An example of this is Israeli seizure of the West Bank from Jordan during the Six Day War.
2. *Annexation*: When one political entity unilaterally extends its sovereignty over a piece of territory. The primary agent of change is diplomacy, although a threat of force may be implicit. An example of this process is France's acquisition of the Saar from Germany after World War II.
3. *Cession*: When part of a political entity is yielded to another entity through plebiscite, purchase, treaty, compensating agreement, or as a consequence of hostilities. An example of this is the transfer of the Fernando Po from the United Kingdom to Spain in 1843.
4. *Secession*: When an existing entity is dissolved or modified as a result of one or more parts of the entity leaving that entity in order to establish a new independent entity or entities.[16] The creation of Bangladesh in 1971 is an example of secession.
5. *Unification*: When a new political entity forms out of two or more preexisting entities.[17] The combination of Prussia and various provinces in the 1860s forming the German state is an example of this process.
6. *Mandated Territory*: When a territorial unit is placed under the control of a political entity by an international organization (that is, League of Nations, United Nations). An example of this is the mandate given to Australia over Nauru (a former German possession) after World War I.
7. *Independence Granted*: When colonial rule over a dependency is terminated. This termination must involve the former dependency attaining effective control over its own foreign affairs and armed forces as well as achieving some measure of diplomatic recognition (for example, India).

Table 2.4 Process of Territorial Change

Process	Percentage of Total	Number
Conquest	15.6	120
Annexation	14.5	112
Cession	42.3	326
Secession	4.8	37
Unification	4.8	37
Mandate	2.5	19
Independence	15.5	119

The predominant process of change is cession, the method for 42 percent of the cases. This indicates that most territorial changes are formalized by treaty, sometimes as the result of military conflict and other times through peaceful negotiation. Apparently, the chaotic process of earlier times, when explorers charted new territory and made competing claims, has been replaced by a degree of order and a rule of law in many transfers of territories. Also apparent from Table 2.3 are the relatively few instances of secession or unification; political entities rarely split apart or merge in the state-making process. In the contemporary era, there has been a marked resistance to changing political boundaries to unite two states or to break up existing entities (except for the creation of Bangladesh) in order to satisfy nationalistic demands for autonomy.

In this chapter, we have charted the territorial history of the international system with particular reference to the growth in the number and configuration of nation-states. Analyses on the number of states, population, and area in the international system were presented. We also looked at transfers of territorial sovereignty between states along several dimensions. Chapter 3 provides an empirical analysis of the conditions for military conflict in our first subset of cases, namely those involving the creation of new members of the international system.

Notes

1. V.I. Lenin, *Imperialism: The Highest Stage of Capitalism* (New York: International Publishers, 1939); Joseph Schumpeter, *History of Economic Analysis* (New York: Oxford University Press, 1964).
2. See Stephen Krasner, ed., *International Regimes* (Ithaca: Cornell University Press, 1982).
3. The list of nation-states is taken from Melvin Small and J. David Singer, *Resort to Arms* (Beverly Hills, Calif.: Sage Publications, 1982).
4. There is a distinction that must be kept in mind between *gaining independence* and *entering the international system*. Because our study begins in 1816, these two are usually synonymous, as most new states after 1816 pass through the intermediate stage of being a colony. Nevertheless, there are cases in which a state directly enters the international system. The most dramatic example of this is Japan. Thus, to our original territorial change data set, we have added 4 cases of direct entry into the system. In addition, there are 21 cases of *states* becoming independent, but not entering the international system. States have on occasion lost territorial control to local groups that never established themselves as recognized states. For example, several South African provinces briefly left British control. Thus, we loosely speak of independence as equivalent to entering the international system, but all analyses are based on actual entries, be they direct or the result of independence from imperial/colonial domination.
5. This is not to say that some territories (for example, China in the nineteenth century) were merely empty spaces on the map. Rather, they were not encompassed in the grouping of states we call the international system.
6. One extreme outlier was removed from these calculations. Its inclusion resulted in a correlation coefficient of around .98.
7. Nevertheless, recent events in Europe may lead to the creation of new states or the consolidation or reappearance of old ones (for example, Lithuania).
8. The list of territorial changes is taken from a data set of the Correlates of War Project, collected and coded by Philip Schaefer. A description of that data set was initially reported in Paul Diehl and Gary Goertz, "Territorial Changes and Militarized Conflict," *Journal of Conflict Resolution* 32 (1988):103–122. Since then, we have altered some of the coding schemes, filled in some of the missing data, and recoded some of the variables, particularly the variable related to the incidence of military conflict. Thus, astute readers may notice differences in the numbers reported in this book versus those reported in the aforementioned article. We did not make an attempt to check the entire data set nor did we seek to identify possible omissions. The Correlates of War Project plans a systematic revision of the data set in the 1990s. For information on the variables and their coding, see Philip Schaefer, Gary Goertz, and Paul F. Diehl, "Territorial Change Coding Manual" (Ann Arbor, Mich.: Correlates of War Project mimeo, 1990).
9. Nazli Choucri and Robert North, *Nations in Conflict* (San Francisco: W.H. Freeman, 1975).

10. Charles Gochman and Zeev Maoz, "Militarized Interstate Disputes, 1816–1976: Procedures, Patterns, and Insights," *Journal of Conflict Resolution* 28 (1984):592–594.
11. Figure 2.5 is calculated with only the 160 cases of homeland territorial changes that involved states on both sides of the exchange instead of the full 209 cases. This was largely done because the subset of 160 forms the basis for the analysis in chapter 4. In any case, the patterns are not substantially different from those including the other 49 cases.
12. Because of the difficulty in estimating the population of the territorial units affected, over a third of the cases have *missing data*. When the area exchanged was very small and exact data were not available, the size was recorded as one square kilometer.
13. Gochman and Maoz, 609.
14. In some cases, there is *dual use* of land areas in which the control over the land is not zero-sum. For example, the lease on Guantanamo Naval Base allows the United States exclusive use of that area despite the retention of territorial possession by Cuba.
15. One observation was removed because its inclusion made the resulting calculation inaccurate as a description of the situation in general; including that case resulted in a correlation of .97.
16. Attempts by dependencies to gain independence are not included under secession even if the mother country considers such dependencies to be part of the metropole (for example, Algeria or Angola).
17. When armed force is involved, the change is coded as a *conquest* if there was no formal treaty transferring the territory.

CHAPTER 3

Entering International Society: Military Conflict and State Formation

In the previous chapter, we noted that the number of states in the international system has grown seven-fold since the Congress of Vienna. Virtually all of the new system members passed through a transitional stage of being a dependent territory under the domination of a major power. Over time, the imperial/colonial empires of Britain, France, and others withered away, and the number of new Third World states increased dramatically. Yet, the transition from subjugated territory to independent state was not always smooth or peaceful. In this chapter, we set out to model the conditions under which military conflict occurs in the subset of territorial changes involving national independence.[1] We hypothesize that the power status of the imperial/colonial state, the importance of the territory to that state, and norms in international society condition whether the transfer of sovereignty involves military conflict or not.

In one sense, state formation represents the most basic form of territorial changes: an indigenous population achieves self-determination. Nevertheless, the situation is rarely that simple. National independence can have dramatic consequences for the imperial/colonial power, other states, and the global community. Three instances come to mind to illustrate this point. First, the League of Nations assigned Palestine as a mandate territory under the guardianship of Great Britain. Massive Jewish immigration after World War II, fueling Jewish–Arab tensions, complicated the various plans for independence put forward by the British and the United Nations. When the British mandate expired and the new Israeli state was established, it immediately touched off a war in the Middle East that foreshadowed over 40 years of conflict to come. The awkward transition to independence in Palestine created circumstances that remain major threats to world peace today.

Second, when a nation gains its independence, the implications of that event are not inherently confined to the states in the immediate area. The difficult transition of Indo-Chinese states to independence from French colonial domination would trap France and then the United States into fighting with national groups seeking self-determination and political power. Had the circumstances and methods by which Vietnam gained independence been different, for example, the history of bloodshed in Southeast Asia that continues today might have been avoided. Third and finally, the method of granting independence can also be hazardous to the stability of the imperial/colonial power. French policy toward Algeria produced both discontent among native Algerians as well as among French nationals living in the territory. An army revolt almost succeeded in gaining control of the colony and threatened the stability of the de Gaulle government. This illustrates that the method of granting national independence can also be hazardous to the stability of the imperial/colonial power.

State formation is, therefore, interesting in its own right as one aspect of the study of conflict. It is also critical in influencing a wide range of other international political events. The creation of new states has precipitated the intermittent wars and persistent conflict in the Middle East and Africa as well as the United States' involvement in the longest war of its history.

Although the size of the international system has not grown substantially since the peak growth rate in the early 1960s, the issue of national independence is still a salient one and will likely continue to be so in the future. Various national and subnational groups around the globe seek autonomy or independence for their people. Forty-three dependent territories of various sizes and locations remain as of this writing.[2] Several Pacific islands and Puerto Rico are also areas where nationalist movements calling for independence exist. Indeed, the independence movement in New Caledonia was a factor in the last French presidential elections. In still other regions, separatist movements advocate independence for their national or ethnic groups. In the past 25 years, such movements have arisen in places as diverse as Canada (in Quebec), Sri Lanka, and the

Soviet Union. The conditions under which these possible future territorial changes will involve military conflict is uncertain and the mechanisms by which the transitions to independence can be completed peacefully are as yet unknown. We hope to shed some light on these concerns in the following pages.

The theoretical significance of this analysis is twofold. First, the results of this chapter can ascertain if and when military conflict occurs during the process of national independence; this is a largely unexplored area of conflict research. Second, uncovering the conditions for violence in national independence is potentially a vital theoretical link to understanding all forms of interstate conflict. Maoz argues that the process by which new states are formed affects their subsequent conflict behavior.[3] His findings indicate that state formation processes that involved intense and violent struggles between indigenous populations and imperial/colonial powers increase the likelihood that the resulting new state will be involved in future militarized disputes.

In the next section, we trace the empirical patterns of territorial changes involving state formation, with special attention to their frequency across time and space. We then proceed to specify our own theoretical and statistical model of military conflict and national independence. The final sections of this chapter include an attempt to test that model and a discussion of the results.

Empirical Patterns

Previously we noted that the growth of the international system, of which national independences are part, was distributed unevenly over time. The patterns are similar for cases of national independence, as noted in Figure 3.1.

Most of the independences are clustered in the period immediately following World War II. It seems as if a dependent territory must go through several phases before it becomes a candidate for independence. An initial phase occurs when an imperial/colonial power assumes control of the territory. During that time, the dominant state will be highly resistant to any attempts at giving up power; furthermore, it is unlikely that any indigenous groups will exist or that they will not be sufficiently organized to demand independence. A middle phase is when the dependent territory yields maximum economic benefits for the sovereign and the situation remains stable. A third phase might be when the economic returns diminish or flatten out and the local population begins to demand self-determination. This may culminate in a sudden, and sometimes violent, independence or a transition period in which preparations are made for the transfer of power from the imperial/colonial master to the new, indigenous regime.

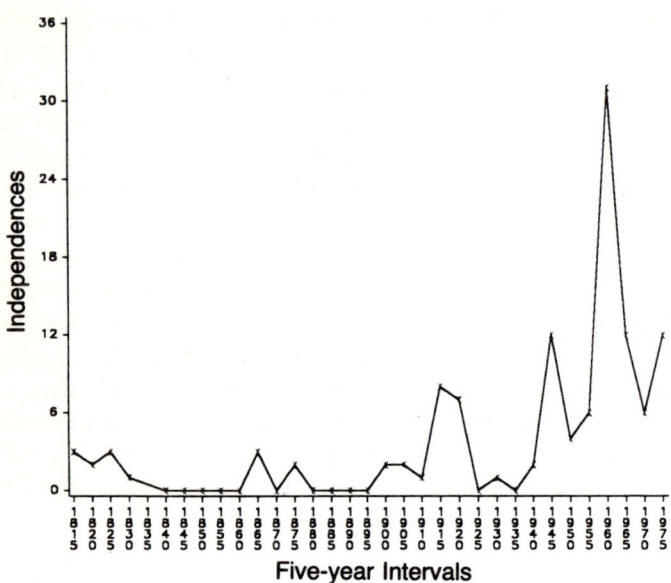

Figure 3.1 Independences Over Time

The entire process can be a lengthy one. Many of the "new" states were former dependent territories acquired in the nineteenth century; it took well into the twentieth century, with a little assistance from the World Wars, to go through all phases. Perhaps then it is not surprising that many of our cases are skewed in the direction of the middle twentieth century. An exception to this is the independence of South American states which took place in the nineteenth century, a lengthy period after their initial colonization by Spain. The effect of the time of the first colonization on subsequent independence is further evident when one looks at the regional distribution of state formation cases.

Table 3.1 Regional Distribution of National Independences

Region	19th Century	20th Century	Total
Americas	9	12	21
Europe	5	14	19
Africa	0	44	44
Middle East	0	16	16
Asia	0	21	21

Table 3.1 shows the distribution of independence cases according to region and stratified by century. Independence in the Western Hemisphere occurs prior to World War I; the exceptions are those states in the Caribbean that do not achieve their independence until a generation or two later. Many states in this hemisphere, particularly those on the South American continent, became dependent territories in the sixteenth and seventeenth centuries. In contrast, dependent territories on the Asian and African continents were acquired much later, many in the late nineteenth century. Accordingly, the later acquired dependent territories were also those that achieved independence in the past 40 years. Europe has slightly more than a dozen cases of independence in the twentieth century, but these are primarily confined to the time between the world wars. Those new states were not former colonies, but rather components of states that included heterogeneous ethnic and national groups.

In seeking to understand the conditions for military conflict in these cases, an important consideration is the yielding state or former sovereign of the territory. Table 3.2 lists the states most involved as the yielding side as well as some indicators of the area and population lost over the period of study. The United Kingdom and France easily top the list as the dominant colonial powers of the last two centuries; collectively, these two states are involved in over half of the cases studied. Other states, such as the Netherlands and Portugal, also had far-flung colonial possessions, but by the nineteenth century most had been relinquished to other states. The sheer magnitude of French and British losses is evident by comparing their current holdings with what they have given up. The area given up by the United Kingdom is 132 times greater than the current size of the British homeland. Correspondingly, the population of the current "British Empire" is less than one-tenth the size of the population it has given up in the past century and a half. France has given up an area 20 times as great as it now controls with a resulting loss of population of over 60 percent. The British Commonwealth and the French–African ties have replaced the system of political domination before 1945.

Table 3.2 States Most Involved in Independence Cases

State	Number	Total Population	Mean Population	Total Area	Mean Area
United Kingdom	47	614,595	13,076	32,508	692
France	24	93,944	3,914	10,670	445
Spain	7	14,266	2,038	7,738	1,105
Portugal	6	20,049	3,342	10,332	1,722
Ottoman Emp. /Turkey	6	12,924	2,154	520	86
Russia/U.S.S.R.	5	23,188	4,637	866	173
Netherlands	4	78,951	19,738	1,685	421
Belgium	3	20,005	6,668	2,399	800

Population reported in thousands.
Area reported in thousand square kilometers.

It might be noted that the population figures in Table 3.2 can be a little misleading. States that gave up their dependent territories before 1945, such as Spain, will tend to have lower lost population figures than those that relinquished territory after the Second World War; the overall growth in world population in this century and particularly in the past forty years may make direct comparisons of population figures problematic. Furthermore, one independence, such as India in 1947, could skew the total and average population figures. In this way, the area figures listed may be more enlightening as to the significance of the losses for the former imperial/colonial powers.

The Conditions for Military Conflict

The transition from dependent territory to independent state is not always a peaceful one. Many imperial/colonial powers are unwilling to give up the economic and political benefits that emanate from control over a particular territory. In the 121 cases of national independence, approximately 20 percent of them involved some military conflict within a year prior to the date of actual independence. From a historical point of view, the incidence of conflict is not spread evenly across the period of study.

Figure 3.2 shows the percentage of cases involving military conflict across five-year blocks of history. Because of the limited number of cases in the nineteenth century, the most useful analysis comes from looking at the twentieth century cases, especially those after 1945. There is a greater propensity for conflict, not surprisingly, surrounding the World Wars. Yet, as the frequency of territorial changes has increased in the post-World War II era, the frequency of conflict has declined. In the model that we design and test below, we hope to account for this peculiar pattern.

Figure 3.2 Military Conflict and National Independence

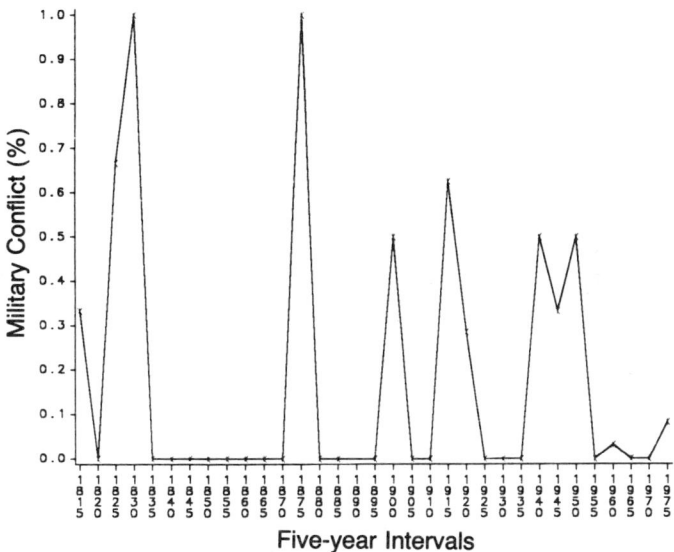

What conditions make the likelihood of violence greater and which allow the peaceful transition of dependent territories to independent state? The decision to use military force rests, in our view, on the willingness of the imperial/colonial power to surrender sovereignty peacefully. At first, it seems logical that any model of military conflict should include information about both sides, in this case about indigenous forces. If there is a movement for independence, however, then the imperial/colonial power has the choice to grant that request or resist it with military force. The existence of organized indigenous military forces almost by definition means that there was military conflict; thus, indigenous forces are perfectly correlated with military conflict. Also, an imperial/colonial power may grant self-determination before the local population wants or is even ready for independence, or before there is an organized local opposition. It must be remembered that the population of cases is confined to successful independences, not including instances in which indigenous forces tried and failed to throw out the imperial/colonial government. When a dependent territory is granted independence, the conditions of that transition (peaceful or violent) are largely determined by the actions of the imperial/colonial power and not by indigenous forces.

Drawing on the theoretical framework in the first chapter, we see three sets of factors that may influence the willingness of the imperial/colonial power to relinquish the territory without a fight. Traditional, realpolitik models have focused on power and other national attributes as determinants of state behavior. Although we regard such factors as significant, we believe that there are other influences on state behavior that are not yet reflected in the academic literature on international conflict. Therefore, in addition to the strength of the imperial/colonial power, we also look to the importance of the territory and the prevailing norms in the international system as factors influencing the willingness of states to use military force.

The first set of factors relates to the importance of the territory in question. In our view, imperial/colonial powers will be more reluctant to give up territory, and resist calls for national self-determination with military force, if the land is perceived to be valuable. As the reader may recall from the first chapter, territorial importance has two dimensions: intrinsic and relational. With respect to the former in this case, we refer to the economic value that the territory holds for the sovereign. In contrast, relational importance concerns the less tangible value that is attached to the territory by the sovereign because of historical or geographic reasons.

The imperial/colonial power would seem more willing to bear the economic, human, and political costs of military force when the continued territorial control yields benefits that outweigh those costs. Thus, our expectation is that the greater the intrinsic and relational importance of the territory in question, the more likely the transition to independent state will involve military conflict.

Although we believe territorial importance conditions the likelihood of military conflict, we do not think it is the only influence. A second component in the equation for military conflict is the status of the imperial/colonial power. If the imperial/colonial state is increasing in strength, it can probably resist successfully any attempts (through economic and military actions) to take away its territorial possessions by force; any cases of national independence are likely completed with the peaceful consent of the imperial/colonial power. In contrast, an imperial/colonial power on the decline is more vulnerable to nationalist movements. Overextension of territorial control may complicate the state's ability to secure its possessions.[4] The ability to manage problems in its territorial possessions is also correspondingly lessened. This time of uncertainty may prompt the imperial/colonial power to resist any actions that may further contribute to its economic and political decline; the loss of territory would constitute such an event. Furthermore, in times of decline, other states compete for control over these areas or hegemony in the system. The independence movements after World War II are related, in our view, to the rise of the United States as a hegemonic power, at the expense of the United Kingdom and France. Our expectation therefore is, ceteris paribus, military conflict in cases of national independence is more likely when the imperial/colonial power is declining in its power as opposed to being in a period of ascendancy.

The third component in the model of military conflict is the influence that the international system and the community of nations exercises on the imperial/colonial power. Here, it is the presence of a norm that endorses national self-determination through peaceful means. We noted in chapter 1 that such a norm could arise domestically through the repeated experience of losing dependent territory. The norm may also arise from the behavior of other states and from formal resolutions and pronouncements from international bodies. In the next section, we attempt to construct some operational measures of a decolonization norm. Suffice to say here, however, that the willingness of states to resist national movements will be less when there is international pressure to relinquish dependent territorial holdings.

Overall, we expect that military conflict in national independence will be most prevalent in situations that (1) involve dependent territory that is regarded as valuable by the imperial/colonial state, (2) involve an imperial/colonial state in a period of relative power decline, and (3) include a weak norm of national self-determination or none at all. In the next section, we describe the operational indicators for these factors and specify the measurement models used in the analysis.

Measurement Models

In the previous section, we specified the broad set of variables that comprise our model of military conflict in cases of national independence. Yet, while the notion of importance may be conceptually clear, the development of an operational measure of it can be problematic; this is particularly difficult when there are few tangible reference points. Thus, the purpose of this section is to specify the operational indicators used to represent the concepts of importance, power decline, and norms. For each concept, we employ multiple indicators in order more fully to capture the underlying dimension. We also discuss the techniques we use to combine these indicators into one integrated measure of each concept.

IMPORTANCE

In seeking to measure territorial importance, we begin with the strategy of separating intrinsic from relational importance. As noted earlier, these are distinct dimensions of the overall concept. Furthermore, we speculate that the two dimensions of importance have differential effects on the willingness of the imperial/colonial power to use military conflict. Thus, we develop separate indicators for each dimension and keep them distinct in the remainder of the analysis.

Intrinsic importance relates to the value that territory has for all parties in a territorial dispute. With that in mind, we are drawn to indicators that represent permanent or quasi-permanent attributes of a land area; in addition, these attributes must represent some value that is attached to them. Accordingly, our first indicator of intrinsic importance is the physical size of the area involved in the territorial change.[5] The size of the land area stands for a broad set of values that the territory might have. For instance, the size of an area is related to its productive capacity, its natural resources, and its potential for accommodating additional population.

However, a given land area may be arid and barren, in which case the size of the area alone may be a misleading indicator of its intrinsic importance. Therefore, as another indicator of the intrinsic importance of a territory, we look to the population directly affected by the transfer of sovereignty. Additional people provide a state with new sources of labor for economic or military purposes. To indicate intrinsic importance, we use the size of the territory involved in the territorial change and the number of people living in the territory at the time of the change. The number of people living in the territory was often difficult to estimate, particularly in cases in which part of the population fled the area during the fighting. We used population estimates at the date of transfer rather than those prior to any military conflict over territory.

Relational importance refers to the different significance attached to the territory by the parties in the territorial exchange. It is essential then to develop indicators that have the potential for variation between the parties and across territorial disputes. Because our theoretical focus is on the imperial/colonial power in this set of cases (in later chapters we will be concerned with both sides in the exchange), we concentrate on indicators of the importance attached to the territory by that state. Thus, we look at trade flows between the dependent territory and the mother country. The volume of imports and exports gives some sense of the economic ties and benefits that exist for the imperial/colonial power vis-à-vis the territory in question.[6] In order to measure that importance in the context of the imperial/colonial power's whole economy, we look at imports and exports with the colonial possession as a percentage of the mother country's total trade; this shows how important the territory in question is relative to other dependent territories but also how significant (or insignificant) it is to the health of the imperial/colonial power's economy. Thus, our two indicators of relational importance are imports and exports from the territory.

Initially we had thought of including the geographic proximity of the territory to the imperial/colonial state as another indicator of relational importance; the logic is that states will regard areas closer to home as more important than those farther away. Yet, most of the territories involved in this subset of territorial changes are quite distant from the imperial/colonial state. We also believe that the importance of dependent territories is defined more by their economic value than by their military/strategic value (with a few exceptions). Furthermore, the presence of the geographic proximity variable empirically did not form a coherent unity with the trade indicators and perturbed other aspects of model estimation. For these reasons, we did not include the proximity variable in our final measurement model of relational importance.

POWER DECLINE

The second set of indicators is used to model the concept of power decline by the imperial/colonial power. We face two separate concerns: measuring the power of a state and then ascertaining the degree of decline (if any) in that power over time. The problems with the first task are those that have plagued international relations scholars for years. Power is clearly a dynamic, intangible relationship that is not open to direct empirical observation or measurement. As a solution to the problem, scholars have looked at the capabilities (which some call potential power) as a surrogate for power; in effect, power is inferred from capability. We adopt a similar strategy by considering three indicators of a state's capabilities, with special emphasis on the military dimension.

The capabilities in which we are most interested are those related to the ability of a state to exercise influence through military means. Accordingly, we look at three indicators. A state's military expenditures and the number of people in its military are two conventional measures of the military capabilities available for use. Because military power also has a strong economic dimension (a large economy must be available to support sustained military action), we also look at the aggregate strength of the imperial/colonial power's economy using GNP.[7] Yet, using military expenditures, military personnel, and GNP in absolute terms might be misleading. Over time, the capabilities of states have increased, complicating the analysis and the inferences drawn from it in a study with a long temporal domain, such as this one. Furthermore, all power is relative to some countervailing configuration of power.

The appropriate referent group is other imperial/colonial states (usually major powers). The theoretical frameworks, noted in the first chapter, on which we justify the inclusion of the power decline variable, consider such decline vis-à-vis other "peer" states. In many instances, these other states were rivals for imperial/colonial domination of dependent territories. For example, Britain and France were rivals for dependent territory in Africa. Furthermore, a comparison with indigenous forces (if such forces existed and could be comparably measured) would show little variation even after dramatic increases in those forces; the imperial/colonial state is so much more powerful that such increases in indigenous forces or declines in capability of the imperial/colonial state would be barely discernible. Finally, as noted above, the existence of indigenous forces is coterminous with military conflict, making the use of indigenous forces as the referent group inappropriate. Our measure of capabilities calculates the percentage of the total imperial/colonial system capabilities (the sum of capabilities for all imperial/colonial powers) on each respective indicator (military expenditures, military personnel, and GNP) held by the imperial/colonial power in question.[8]

Having specified our indicators of power, we now must explain how we plan to assess decline in that power. We will compare the capabilities of the state in question at the time of the territorial exchange[9] with its capabilities ten years prior to that date. This gives us some short-term indication of whether the imperial/colonial power is experiencing relative decline, stability, or ascendancy, as well as the magnitude of those trends.

NORMS

The last set of indicators relates to a norm favoring the peaceful transition of dependent territories to independent states, or the norm of decolonization. We noted above that the norm derives from national and international experiences. Not surprisingly, then, we use indicators to reflect the rise of norm for each imperial/colonial power, as well as the norm operating for the international system as a whole. Similar to power, the idea of a norm is difficult to quantify. Yet, we believe that by looking at regular patterns of behavior, we can derive a good measure of the phenomenon.

Domestically, there are movements that support self-determination in dependent territories, and the attitude of elites is critical to widespread acceptance of the norm. What will influence broad acceptance of the norm are the prior patterns of behavior with respect to national independence. The extent to which the state becomes accustomed to territories gaining their independence is related to the extent to which the norm has been established and strengthened. Our first indicator is the number of previous cases of independence experienced by the imperial/colonial power. The more times that the state has granted independence, the more accepted giving up dependent territory will be in society. A second indicator is the proportion of previous independences that included military conflict. The more that an imperial/colonial power has peacefully transferred power to a dependent territory in the past, the less likely it will feel an obligation to resist with military force future efforts at decolonization.

Norms at the system level are the product of the norms and behavior of its members. Thus, we use the same two indicators as above (the percentage of independences involving military conflict and the number of previous independences) to measure the development of a decolonization norm at the international level. The exception here is that we not only look at the behavior of the one imperial/colonial power in question, but rather the behaviour of all states. Thus, the indicators are the total number of previous independences in the international system and the proportion of previous cases involving military conflict.

Our measure of norms gives them an interactive relationship with the behavior they are supposed to influence. Unlike incremental models of behavior that seek to predict behavior at time t from actions or situations at $t-1$, we look to the whole history of imperial/colonial behavior since 1816 until time t. The actions of imperial/colonial powers at time t will subsequently affect, but not define completely, the strength of the norms variable at $t+1$ and, accordingly, the willingness of states to relinquish dependent territories peacefully.

Table 3.3 summarizes the various factors that are thought to influence the likelihood of military conflict in cases of national independence and their operational indicators. The next section details the techniques we use to combine those indicators so that we have one measure of each underlying concept.

COMBINING DIMENSIONS

One strategy in our analysis is to consider the indicators separately, assessing each one's ability to predict military conflict in a territorial change. Such an approach, however, would lead to mixed, and sometimes confusing, results at best, as a high score on one indicator for a particular case (for example, area or military personnel) may be offset by relatively low scores on the other indicators (for example, population or GNP). Statistical problems resulting from multicollinearity between the variables in other cases might render any inferences drawn from the results misleading. Furthermore, we have argued that our indicators individually capture only a portion of the underlying dimension they are designed to measure; that is, population size measures only one component of the intrinsic importance of a territory. Therefore, we attempt the measurement of our concepts by integrating the indicators into one combined measure.

In order to integrate the indicators, we employ the LISREL statistical modeling technique.[10] LISREL is used for structural equation models in which multiple indicators are used to measure the variables in the model (in this case, intrinsic and relational importance, power decline, and norms); the relationships between those variables are then estimated (here we are concerned with the relationship of those variables to military conflict). We first specify the concepts of importance (intrinsic and relational), power decline, and norms (national and international) as latent variables. We then use confirmatory factor analysis among the measured indicators (for example, area and population) in order to estimate the latent variables (for example, intrinsic importance).

Table 3.3 Summary of Variables and Indicators

Latent Variable	Indicator	Operational Measure
Intrinsic Importance	Area	Size of territory exchanged in square kilometers
	Population	Number of people living in the territory at the time of the exchange

Table 3.3 continued

Relational Importance	Imports	Volume of imports between the territory and the colonial power as a percentage of the colonial power's total imports
	Exports	Volume of exports between the territory and the colonial power as a percentage of the colonial power's total exports
Power Decline	Military Expenditures	Change in military spending from $t-10$ to t as a proportion of total system spending
	Military Personnel	Change in military personnel from $t-10$ to t as a proportion of total system military personnel
	GNP	Change in GNP from $t-10$ to t as a proportion of total system GNP
Norms	Previous Independence Cases—Nation	Number of previous independence cases experienced by the colonial power
	Previous Incidence of Military Conflict—Nation	Proportion of previous independence cases experienced by the colonial power that involved military conflict
	Previous Independence Cases—System	Number of previous independence cases in the international system
	Previous Incidence of Military Conflict—System	Proportion of previous independence cases in the international system that involved military conflict

There are several benefits from the use of LISREL here. First, we gain a better developed, and we believe more accurate, measure of the underlying concepts of importance, power decline, and norms. Rather than rely on a single indicator that may capture only one dimension of the concepts, we use several indicators that tap multiple dimensions. Using several indicators in a LISREL context permits us not to separate the measurment aspects from the regression (structural) aspects of the model. It permits us to say that, given our structural model, our indicators of the latent variables are coherent and that we are in fact tapping the underlying concept. In addition, unlike other studies that use multiple indicators, we also empirically estimate each indicator's impact on the final measure.[11] The final indexes provide single, multidimensional, and interval measures of the three concepts. Second, LISREL is particularly valuable in deriving measures of intangible concepts such as norms or importance that cannot be measured directly. Finally, the estimates of the parameters of the measurement models give us some idea of how well the latent variables are measured rather than assuming a priori that the measurement error is negligible, as is always the case when a single indicator is used.

The outcome variable, military conflict, is measured dichotomously. If independence was accompanied by fighting between organized forces on both sides (indigenous and colonial military forces) within one year of the actual independence, then the transfer is considered to involve military conflict. All other cases are coded as not involving military conflict.[12]

Empirical Results

The results of the complete analysis are given in Figure 3.3. The discussion of the measurement models cannot be disassociated from the estimation of the entire model, but the majority can be considered independently.

MEASUREMENT MODELS

The measurement models assumed the errors of measurement (the extreme left portion of Figure 3.3) are independent, and there was no compelling theoretical or empirical reason to change this assumption in the course of the analysis. Because there are at least two measured variables for each latent variable, the model is identified and thus the parameter estimates are unique. The correlation matrix was analyzed because the dependent variable is dichotomous for which LISREL estimates polyserial correlation (correlation coefficients between continuous variables and discrete ordinal ones); hence, the coefficients in Figure 3.3 are standardized.

We now turn our attention to how strongly the indicators are related to the latent variable that they are supposed to capture. The power decline variable consists of three components: the decline in economic power represented by GNP and the decline in military power represented by changes in military expenditures and military personnel respectively. The latent variable is more related to the military than to the economic aspects of power decline. The numbers in parentheses are the R^2 values between the indicators and latent variables (with a maximum value of 1). It is with the military personnel measure that the power decline variable is most associated ($R^2=.91$); the strength of association is somewhat less for the other two indicators. Overall, however, the measurement model for the power decline variable is well specified with almost 50 percent of the variance accounted for with each indicator (a good result by social science standards).

We postulated above that a norm for peaceful transition to independence had two components—an international norm and a national one. These were initially independently estimated, but the resulting unmeasured variables were highly correlated (.91). We decided to collapse the national and international components into one latent norm variable. The indicators of this norm, the number of previous independences and the percentage of those involving military conflict—both by nation and system-wide—are in general strongly related to the latent variable (note the R^2 values ranging from .37 to .82). The relationships are in the predicted directions: as the norm of independence becomes established by nations becoming independent, the percentage of military conflict decreases (hence the negative signs for $-.85$ and $-.61$). The relationships are stronger for the international indicators, as individual nations follow this norm with varying degrees of resistance, as evidenced by the relatively low value ($R^2=.37$) for the percentage of military conflict by nation indicator. Nevertheless, at the system level the

Figure 3.3 LISREL Model of Military Conflict and National Independence

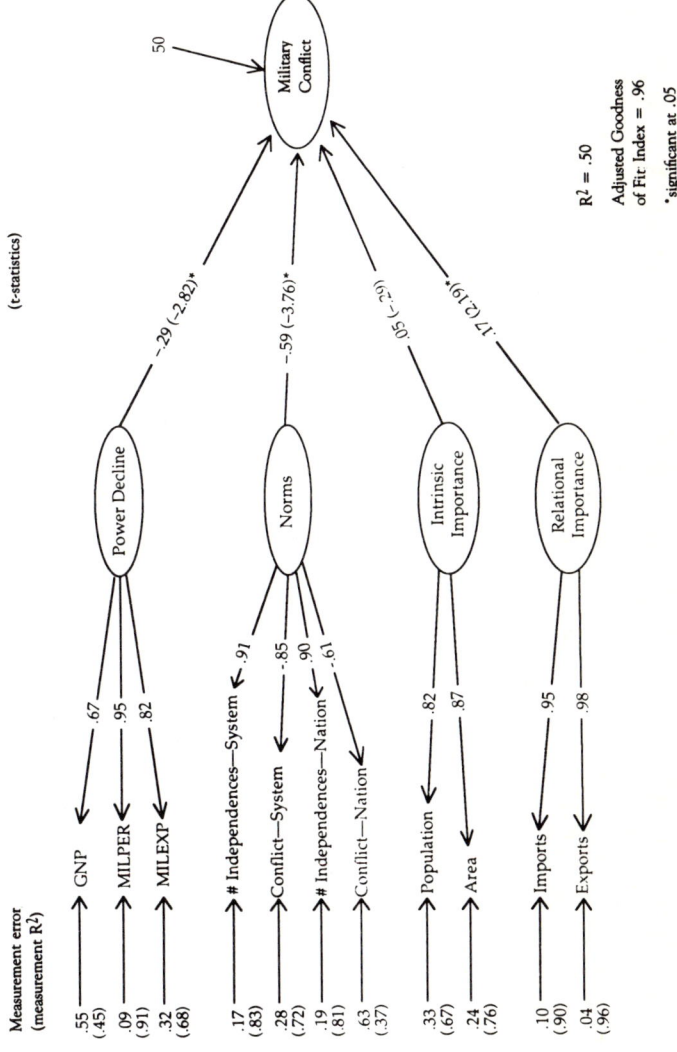

aggregate experience of all nations is highly related to the norm variable, as evidenced by the high R^2 value of .72 for the military conflict indicator. Again, the results of the measurement were quite successful with an acceptable amount of measurement error.

The measurement models for the latent importance variables were also well specified. The trade indicators, imports and exports, yielded high R^2 values of .90 and .96 respectively for relational importance. In addition, area and population proved to be good measures of intrinsic importance. Overall, the measurement models were more than satisfactory. The R^2 values were generally quite high, the coefficients were in the expected directions, and the latent variables were not unduly biased toward one indicator over another.

STRUCTURAL EQUATION

Having discussed the measurement of the independent variables, we now consider the estimates of the structural equation, noted in the right hand portion of Figure 3.3. The results reported were obtained with unweighted least squares (ULS) because the variables in this model are generally not normally distributed. The same analyses were performed with maximum likelihood with very similar results.[13]

For those unfamiliar with the structural equation modeling approach, the closest analogy is regression. The four independent variables (relational importance, intrinsic importance, power decline, and norms) are used to explain whether a case of national independence will involve military conflict or not. If the model is properly specified, the variables' coefficients will be significant and collectively they will account for most of the variance in the military conflict outcomes (the latter indicated by high R^2 values).

The overall fit of the model as indicated by the R^2 value of .50, or alternatively by the Adjusted Goodness-of-Fit Index (AGFI, which measures how well the variance-covariance matrix matches the one given by the data, adjusted for degrees of freedom of the model), of .96 (maximum = 1) is very good. For a model with only four independent variables and a dichotomous dependent variable, this implies that the relationships are strong. The use of ULS does not permit significant tests for the coefficients of each variable, but maximum likelihood does and we use its t-statistics as evidence for the significance of the coefficients; the maximum likelihood estimates were close to the unweighted least squares estimates (this is evidence of the stability of the relationship). The t-statistics for the structural part of the model are given in parentheses toward the right hand part of Figure 3.3. Of the four independent variables, three have significant t-statistics. Only the intrinsic importance of the territory appears unrelated to the outbreak of military conflict in the national independence process.

The coefficients are in the hypothesized direction (positive for the importance variables and negative for the power and norms variables) with the likelihood of military conflict increasing as the imperial/colonial state declines in power, as norms of independence are weakened, and when the territory has economic importance for the imperial/colonial power.

Conclusions

In general, our model was quite successful in explaining the onset of military conflict in cases of national independence, accounting for 50 percent of the variance in outcomes. All the variables were statistically significant influences on the likelihood of military conflict with the exception of the intrinsic importance of the territory in question.

Traditional, realpolitik models have focused on the attributes of states or the international system to account for the incidence of military conflict. In one sense, our analysis confirms this focus, as the power status of the imperial/colonial state is a significant factor in the onset of military conflict. Yet, two sets of factors (international norms and issue salience or importance) not included in traditional models were also significant influences. One notable finding in comparing the standardized coefficients is that international norms exercise the greatest influence on the chances for military conflict in this set of cases. Realpolitik views emphasize the anarchy of the international system with an accompanying absence of influence from supranational actors. Our results suggest that such a view is too narrow and that understanding military conflict requires consideration of a broad range of factors.

Despite our strong results, we recognize that there are alternative explanations for the rapid decolonization after World War II and the peaceful fashion in which it was conducted. Some may argue that colonialism was no longer necessary for the development of the capitalist world economy. Through investment policies, currency controls, and other neocolonial instruments, imperial/colonial powers could retain the economic benefits of colonialism without the accompanying maintenance costs.[14] Thus, according to this interpretation, the decision to grant independence was made on cost-benefit grounds and not based on some internationally developed moral obligation.

Less credibly, it might also be suggested that military conflict is not less common in attempts at national independence, only less successful in recent times (and therefore the only cases of national independence will be those granted peacefully and voluntarily). Yet, none of the current dependent territories appear to have experienced unsuccessful violent struggles for independence. The only military conflict seems to have occurred when subnational groups, as in Sri Lanka and elsewhere, have tried to create new states of their own.

Of course, there are limitations to inferring motivation from behavior, and we recognize that we cannot say for sure whether states were primarily motivated by the norm to give up their territories or did so for other reasons. This is also not to say that international norms will be important in all contexts. Yet, our analysis does suggest the potential for a well-developed norm to modify state behavior when economic or security concerns might dictate otherwise.

In the next chapter, we look at another subset of territorial change cases, those involving the exchange of home territory by recognized members of the international system. The lack of a strong international norm governing behavior and the inherent emotional and political attachments to homeland territory make these cases more susceptible to military conflict.

Notes

1. In this chapter, we look at all cases of territories gaining their independence *and* joining the international system. This includes most of those listed under *independence* as well as some from other categories in chapter 2. We did not include, however, some anomalies such as the breakup of the United Arab

Republic and the Mali Federation; these were very brief confederations that quickly disintegrated and do not fit the pattern of independence from imperial/colonial powers as do the rest of the cases. Libya is excluded as its independence in 1951 was not achieved from any imperial/colonial power per se (the Italians lost the territory during World War II). Portions of Libya were administered by the French and the British after the war and the agreement to grant independence was achieved through a United Nations resolution.

2. Martin Glassner and Harm de Blij, *Systematic Political Geography*, 4th ed. (New York: John Wiley, 1989).
3. Zeev Maoz, "Joining the Club of Nations: Political Development and International Conflict, 1816–1976," *International Studies Quarterly* 33 (1989):199–231.
4. William Thompson and Gary Zuk, "World Power and the Strategic Trap of Territorial Commitments," *International Studies Quarterly* 30 (1986):249–267.
5. The size of the area is measured in square kilometers.
6. Trading ties have been used in a number of studies to indicate the degree of economic interest by an imperial/colonial or neocolonial power. See Steven Rosen, "The Open Door Imperative and United States Foreign Policy" in *Testing Theories of Economic Imperialism*, eds. Steven Rosen and James Kurth (Lexington, Mass.: D.C. Heath, 1979), 136; John Odell, "Correlates of United States Military Assistance and Military Intervention" in *Testing Theories*, eds. Rosen and Kurth, 150–154; and Robert McKinlay and Richard Little, "The United States Aid Relationship: A Test of the Recipient Need and the Donor Interest Models," *Political Studies* 27 (1979):236–250. Imports and exports are measured in the native currency of the imperial/colonial power.
7. Military expenditure and personnel figures are taken from the Correlates of War Project. Spending figures are standardized in British sterling until 1920 and United States dollars thereafter. GNP figures are taken from Paul Bairoch, "Europe's GNP, 1800–1970," *Journal of European Economic History* 3 (1974):557–608, supplemented by the authors' own estimates; estimates are in US dollars with 1960 as the base year.
8. This is a method used by J. David Singer and his Correlates of War Project colleagues. It has the advantages of making comparisons across various historical exports valid and accounting for the relative character of power. To understand the method in another context, see J. David Singer, Stuart Bremer, and John Stuckey, "Capability Distribution, Uncertainty, and Major Power War, 1820–1965" in *Peace, War, and Numbers*, ed. Bruce Russett (Beverly Hills: Sage Publications, 1972), 25–26 and Stuart Bremer, "National Capabilities and War Proneness" in *The Correlates of War II: Testing Some Realpolitik Models*, ed. J. David Singer (New York: Free Press, 1980), 59–66.
9. In order to be sure that the capabilities are actually available at the time of the exchange, we look at figures for the year prior to the exchange (and hence also ten years before that) rather than the year of the exchange.

This gives a more accurate view of the situation, especially if the exchange occurred prior to the beginning of the fiscal year in a given state.

10. For extensive discussion of the concept as well as the techniques of confirmatory factor analysis and LISREL, see J. Scott Long, *Confirmatory Factor Analysis* (Sage University Paper Series on Quantitative Applications in the Social Sciences, nos. 07–033. Beverly Hills: Sage Publications, 1985) and Leslie Hayduk, *Structural Equation Modeling with LISREL: Essentials and Advances* (Baltimore: Johns Hopkins University Press, 1987).

11. In their study, Singer, Bremer, and Stuckey, "Capability Distribution, Uncertainty, . . ." assign a priori equal weights to their six indicators in forming a composite measure of national capability. In contrast, Ferris weights his indicators according to the squared variance associated with each indicator in an analysis, measuring the contribution of each indicator to the variance in his overall power index; see Wayne Ferris, *The Power Capabilities of Nation-States* (Lexington, Mass.: Lexington Books, 1974) 43–50.

12 Because the dependent variable is dichotomous, the usual approach would be to use probit/logit analysis. In fact, this was attempted, but it proved impossible to reconstruct all the latent variables generated by LISREL for use in such analysis. Thus, an approximation of the probit analysis, a linear analysis using unweighted least squares (ULS), was performed in LISREL. In many previous studies (see Maresh Malhotra, "A Comparison of the Predictive Validity of Procedures for Analyzing Binary Data," *Journal of Business and Economic Statistics* 1 (1983):326–336), the results of linear regression were not normally different from probit; partial probit analyses done with portions of the model confirmed this expectation in this instance. Consistent results were also obtained using maximum likelihood estimates.

13. Minor modifications (changing some error terms, altering the measurement models, and so forth) did not significantly affect the relationships reported.

14. This argument is detailed in Raymond Betts, *Uncertain Dimensions: Western Overseas Empires in the 20th Century* (Minneapolis: University of Minnesota Press, 1985). British inability (in the face of that nation's decline) to sustain the burden of maintaining India as a colony is cited by de Schwernez as the reason for granting India independence after World War II; see Karl de Schwernez, *The Rise and Fall of British India* (New York: Methuen, 1983), 212ff.

CHAPTER 4

Exchanges of Homeland Territory Between States

As noted in the previous chapter, the transition from colonial possession to independent state can be a violent one. Yet, once a state has gained its independence, territorial conflict does not become a distant memory. Established states are not always content within their defined borders. In this chapter, we set out to describe and model the outbreak of military conflict in 160 cases of the exchange of homeland territory between states. We rely on three sets of variables to predict military conflict: the importance of the territory exchanged, the relative capabilities of the two parties, and the expansionist pressures operating on each party. Again, we look only at successful cases of territorial exchange and do not analyze those instances of territorial conflict that result in a reaffirmation of the status quo.

In previous centuries, territorial conflict was often the result of poorly defined boundary lines. In more recent times, the demarcation of national boundaries and the division of the world into established states has made such disputes considerably less frequent (although not uncommon—for example, the recent dispute between Chile and Argentina over the Beagle Channel which was mediated by the Pope). Even though so-called boundary line disputes are less common than in earlier eras, states still seek to acquire control over additional territory for a variety of motivations.

For many states, particularly those relatively new states, territorial expansion is rooted in the process of national development. As a state experiences economic and demographic pressures from increases in population, it may feel the need to acquire new territories in order to relieve those pressures. The United States' drive to the Pacific Ocean in the nineteenth century can be attributed in part to this motivation. Yet, specific economic motives may be at the heart of the territorial expansion. The United States acquisition of what is now the Panama Canal Zone was motivated by the economic benefits of trans-oceanic shipping facilitated by the canal.

Another motivation for territorial expansion is security. Territorial control over a given area may be critical to the national security and defense of a state. Historically, attacks on Russia from the West have occurred through Poland; not surprisingly then, the Soviet desire to dominate Poland is predicated on a strategy for avoiding any repeat of such attacks. More recently, the Israeli annexation of the Golan Heights is rooted in the belief that control over this area will decrease the chances of a sudden attack by its Syrian neighbor.

Beyond economic and security concerns, territorial acquisition can be attributed to the broader goal of regional hegemony. Vietnamese incursions into Cambodia during the 1970s indicated a desire for domination in Southeast Asia. Libya's forays into northern Chad and threats against her neighbors are evidence of Quadaffi's quest for expanding influence in North Africa.

A fourth prominent source of territorial expansion is the quest to unite people of a common ethnic heritage or national origin under the same government. The legacy of many national independence cases was the failure of state territorial boundaries to correspond with less formal national or ethnic boundaries. The result is what Rejai and Enloe have referred to as state-nations (as opposed to the conventional term nation-states), as the establishment of political authority in these states has preceded cultural integration.[1] Some instances of this phenomenon are a result of the colonial heritage of the state. Colonial boundaries, which cut across ethnic groupings, formed the basis for later state boundaries. The boundaries of many African states are the result of this process. Yet, this problem is not only evident among former colonies. The breakup of the Austro-Hungarian Empire has fueled ethnic tensions in that area, the Albania–Yugoslavia disagreements being a typical example. Territorial expansion based on ethnic motivation has erupted throughout modern history; the Ethiopia–Somalia war in the late 1970s is but one recent manifestation of how ethnic concerns can drive territorial conflict. Hitler's move into the Suedetenland, although related to other concerns as well, is a famous example.

Whatever the motivation for territorial expansion, it forms an important component of most interstate conflict. This is not to say that all interstate wars and disputes in the past two centuries have been fought primarily over territorial claims (although a significant number of them have). Rather, interstate conflict usually has either a primary (that is, the main goals are territorial) or latent (that is, the main goals are not territorial, but involve the defense or acquisition of territory) territorial component to it. An example of the former might be the first (1912) and second (1913) Balkan disputes involving Turkey, Serbia, Greece, and Bulgaria just prior to World War I. These disputes centered around Serbian claims for territorial access to the Adriatic Sea and for a portion of Macedonia. Latent territorial concerns were evident in the Fashoda Crisis and the conflict surrounding the status of West Berlin after World War II. Territorial control in those cases was intimately tied to the overall motivations of the disputants. Since 1945, the overwhelming majority of wars have had a significant territorial component.

For those whose interests focus exclusively on United States-Soviet relations, territorial issues may seem a little passé. Yet, the Soviet Union has struggled to keep its many ethnically diverse republics together. Furthermore, a glance at other ongoing rivalries in the world reveals that territorial issues are still very salient.[2] The continuing feud between India and Pakistan involves competing claims over certain areas mixed in with the conflicting regional designs and religions of each state. The Korean question remains one of territorial control as does the continuing Falklands dispute.

Empirical Patterns

As discussed in earlier chapters, other kinds of territorial changes were clustered around the World Wars or were most common in the post-1945 era. A closer look at Figure 2.5 in chapter 2 which shows the distribution of homeland changes involving two states over time, indicates a repetition of some of those same patterns as well as some new ones. The highest peaks are those that surround the World Wars when territorial changes, such as the extension of the Soviet Union's borders westward during World War II, accompanied the conflict, or when they occurred as part of the postwar settlement, such as the adjustments in the Polish border after World War I. Yet, there seems to be heightened activity in territorial transfers at the time of every major power war. The nineteenth century, a time of relatively few exchanges, has a number of exchanges occurring around the times of the Crimean War, the War of Italian Unification, and the Seven Weeks War. Unlike other types of territorial changes, interstate territorial transfers reach their lowest frequency immediately following the periods of high activity; the rate of decline in territorial changes is obviously the greatest at these times, but the absolute numbers of changes are very low, in some instances with only a handful of cases in the five or ten years after the war.

If one adjusts for the effects of major power wars, the frequency of territorial change seems fairly constant over the time period studied, except for the early stages of the Concert of Europe. In this way, recent trends in the frequency of territorial exchange do not appear in the nuclear age markedly different from in earlier epochs. This is in marked contrast to cases of national independence, which showed a dramatic increase after World War II.

Table 4.1 Interstate Territorial Changes by Region and Century

Region	19th Century	20th Century	Total
Americas	18	11	29
Europe	19	53	72
Africa	0	2	2
Middle East	3	26	29
Asia	6	22	28

The spatial distribution of interstate changes, indicated in Table 4.1, shows a strong European concentration. In one regard, this may not seem surprising in that the European continent has been divided into nation-states the longest of any other region; hence, there has been more opportunity for transfers of homeland territory. Yet, many of the states in the Western Hemisphere have been around since the beginning of this century and the number of changes in this region has been appreciably lower than in Europe. In addition, even given that most African states achieved independence only a short time ago, the incidence of interstate transfers is extremely rare. The lack of interstate territorial changes in Africa may be the result of an agreement among the states in that region to respect the colonial boundaries that formed the basis of state boundaries after independence; the Charter of the Organization of African Unity explicitly stipulates respect of current boundaries. Despite some wars over territorial concerns, our figures indicate that this commitment has generally been observed by member states. This leads us back to the question of why Europe has been the predominant arena for territorial transfers. The answer may lie in that a high percentage of the major powers over the last two centuries have been European states.[3] As we noted above, major power wars seemed to be associated with the incidence of territorial change.

In our earlier analyses, it was the major powers that were most involved in territorial changes. Furthermore, incidences of interstate territorial change seem to be coterminous with major power war. Table 4.2 shows, however, the states most involved in interstate territorial changes are not necessarily the major powers. Noticeably absent from the list is the United States, which is only involved in three interstate changes (recall that most of its expansion was into new areas or dependent territories of other states). France is only involved in four changes despite being a major power throughout the time period under study. In contrast, India and Israel have been involved in over twice as many exchanges despite being in existence only four decades. Many of the states most involved were either in wars themselves or were dramatically affected by major power wars; the latter is especially illustrated by the middle European states on the list (for example, Yugoslavia, Poland, and Czechoslovakia).

The two states at the top of the list in Table 4.2 reflect different ends of the expansionist spectrum. Turkey (and its predecessor, the Ottoman Empire) is involved in many territorial transfers, but primarily on the losing side. This reflects the decline of its empire after the Napoleonic Wars. At the other extreme, the Soviet Union (and its predecessor, Russia) has gradually added territory to its holdings. This expansion has occurred under the

Tsars as well as under the communist regime, giving some credence to oft-heard contention that the 1917 revolution did little to alter the expansionist tendencies of Russia. The reader may recall from chapter 2 that the Soviet Union was involved as the losing side in many territorial changes, but the analysis here reveals that such losses were not primarily of homeland territory.

Table 4.2 States Most Involved in Transfers of Homeland Territory

State	Total Changes	Gain	Loss	Area Gained	Area Lost
Russia/U.S.S.R.	26	15	11	1,628	1,217
China	16	6	10	2,483	4,236
Ottoman Empire/ Turkey	15	4	11	34	221
Italy	14	7	7	113	21
Prussia/Germany	12	7	5	74	36
Pakistan	11	6	5	50	160
India	11	5	6	160	48
Japan	11	7	4	3,052	1,574
Yugoslavia	11	8	3	166	10
Israel	10	4	6	62	48
Czechoslovakia	10	4	6	77	61
Poland	10	6	4	149	190

Area reported in thousands of square kilometers.

In the next section, we outline the conditions for military conflict in these territorial transfers using some of the insights gained from our previous analysis as well as some factors peculiar to the interstate exchange of homeland territory.

The Conditions for Military Conflict

In 160 cases of interstate territorial transfer of homeland territory, approximately 30 percent of them involve military conflict between the two parties. Figure 4.1 shows the frequency of military conflict over time.[4]

Figure 4.1 Military Conflict and Interstate Changes

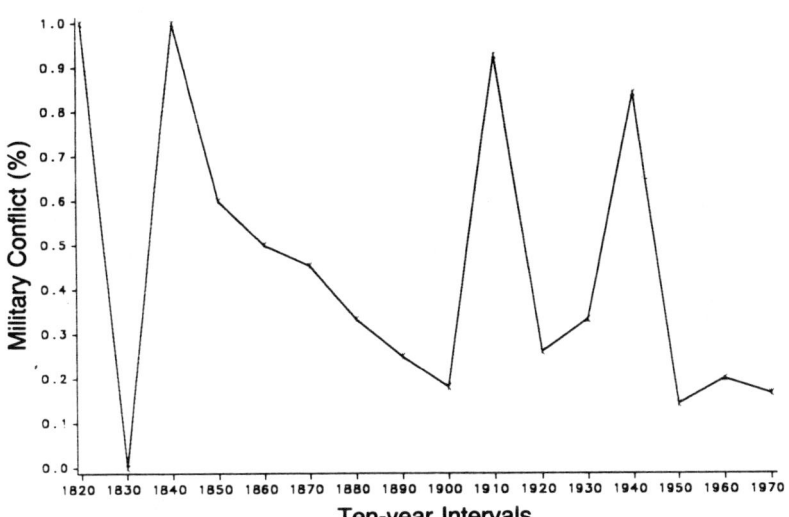

The most notable trend in the frequency of military conflict is a sharp decline in the proportion of violent territorial changes since 1950; this same trend was evident for cases of national independence and territorial changes as a whole. The ability to conquer land areas and incorporate them into the homeland has been severely limited. Many states have tried, most notably Iraq and Argentina in recent times, but the success rate is very low. In that sense, the status quo has been strengthened, and it is very difficult to seize new areas even if the population living there is supportive of such a move. Reinforcing our earlier observation, we note again the decline in the incidence of military conflict following a major power war. Not only are territorial transfers less likely then, but those that do occur are achieved peacefully.

As in our model of the conditions for military conflict in state formation cases and with reference to the theoretical framework of the first chapter, we rely on three sets of factors here to account for militarized conflict between states when they exchanged homeland territory. Unlike our analysis of national independence, however, there needs to be greater attention to the symmetry of preferences and behavior of the two parties. In cases of national independence, our attention was directed to the imperial/colonial power, namely its willingness to give up the territory and its cycle of power. In the cases of interstate territorial transfers, we must devote more attention to the motivations and characteristics of both the gaining and losing sides of the exchange.

The first set of factors, territorial importance, is closely related to our conception in the previous chapter. The intrinsic value of the territory is likely to condition the response of the gaining and losing side to the exchange. We expect that the greater the intrinsic value of the territory involved, the more likely military conflict is to be a part of that transfer. Yet, as we have noted throughout the book, intrinsic importance is only one component of the value that states attach to a particular piece of territory. The relational importance of a territory will also affect the propensity of states to fight over its retention or acquisition. We are concerned with situations in which both parties regard the territory in question as important, only one side does, or neither side does. The first situation is clearly the one in which we expect military conflict to occur. If both sides attach some intangible significance to the territory, this may signal their willingness to fight for it.

The second circumstance, in which only one side regards the territory as important, is expected to be less likely to involve military confrontation. Yet, even within this category of cases, one might expect some variation. We anticipate that if the losing side in an exchange has strong attachment to the territory, the chances for violence are greater than if the acquiring state is the one that values the territory. The inherent costs and uncertainty associated with conflict may make the acquiring state reluctant to risk confrontation; relatively speaking, the acquiring side may pursue territory of this sort that can be garnered without a fight. On the other hand, we postulate that the losing side in the exchange will stubbornly defend territory it regards as important. The underlying assumption is that states are more likely to fight when they have to defend their current homeland as opposed to when they seek to acquire new territory. The final situation, in which neither side attaches much relational importance to the area, is likely to precipitate few instances of military conflict ceteris paribus.

The second set of factors relates to each party's propensity for territorial expansion. Choucri and North use the concept of *lateral pressure* to explain a major power's desire to acquire new, colonial territory and resources in the period from 1870 to 1913.[5] In their conception, the expansionist tendencies of the great powers were bound to clash, producing a competition that was likely to involve military conflict. We offer similar notions for the causes of state expansion into the territorial homeland of other states. If the state acquiring the territory is expanding at the time of the territorial exchange, then it will be more likely to use military force to achieve its ends. Furthermore, the losing state will certainly not concede easily nor peacefully to the *loss* of territory if it is also undergoing pressures for expansion.

We see expansion pressure being driven by two related forces.[6] The first source of pressure can come from increases in population. Increasing population stimulates the need for additional territory, especially in densely populated states, to accommodate the growing population. More importantly, perhaps, population growth increases the economic burden on society, especially in the early stages of growth in that the proportion of the total population that is productive is correspondingly decreased. This can stimulate the need for additional resources that are available with the acquisition of new territory.[7]

Economic pressures form a second source of territorial expansion.[8] Increased economic production produces the twin needs for additional resources to support production and markets for the resulting products. Most states rely on external sources of raw materials, and control over those areas is an easy and reliable way of ensuring availability.[9] Marxist and quasi-Marxist analyses would also point to the need for territorial control to ensure markets for the manufacturing outputs.[10] Overall, when parties to a territorial change are undergoing expansionist pressures, the resulting alterations in boundaries are more likely the product of military conflict than mutual agreement.

In a reevaluation of Choucri and North's work, Zuk argues that the relative capability of a state, not merely the growth of its capabilities, is a better predictor of its territorial expansion and conflict involvement.[11] Thus, the final set of factors involves the relative power distribution between the parties to the territorial exchange. Many border disputes experience protracted latent stages in which few diplomatic or military initiatives are employed to resolve competing claims. The Falklands controversy and competing claims between India and Pakistan have long histories.

Some political geographers suggest that disputes enter their most active phases only after a change in the relative strength of the states involved.[12] Presumably, it is the state that is disadvantaged by the status quo who must gain on its rival before the dispute can become active; the "revisionist" state has the enhanced ability to press its claims. Correspondingly, a change in the power distribution favorable to the status quo state would not apparently prompt a territorial change through violence; by definition, that state has no motivation for altering the currently desirable circumstances. There is conflicting evidence on whether equality in power precipitates more disputes[13] or whether such disputes occur when one state is more powerful and able to press its claims.[14] This mirrors a similar debate on whether preponderance or parity is a more war-prone situation.[15] It is likely that wars occur under a variety of power distributions, so that either extreme view is misleading.[16]

In our set of interstate territorial change cases, we believe that military conflict is more likely when the capability distribution favors the gaining side in the exchange. If the losing side has the advantage, it would only give up territory voluntarily and peacefully. When the gaining side had a significant advantage, it was able to reorder the status quo and either seize or force the relinquishment of the disputed territory through the use of military force. With a capability advantage, it would have viewed the chances for success as quite good.

In summary, we expect that military conflict in interstate transfers is more likely when (1) the territory is regarded as important by both sides, (2) each side experiences expansionist pressures, and (3) there is a significant capability advantage in favor of the gaining side at the time of the exchange. In the next section, we describe the operational indicators for these factors and specify the measurement models used in the analysis.

Measurement Models

IMPORTANCE

In chapter 3, we used multiple indicators to measure the concept of territorial importance. For intrinsic importance, we used the population living in the area and the size of the area as indicators. For relational importance, we used the imports and exports from the territory to the imperial/colonial power as indicators. In the subset of territorial changes involving the exchange of homeland territory, however, such multiple measures were not possible. Because over half of the data on the number of people living in the territory was "missing", we dropped that indicator from the analysis. With respect to relational importance, it is virtually impossible to identify the economic value of the territory involved in exchanges; how one separates the value of the unit exchanged from the state as a whole is uncertain. In addition, the use of geographic proximity measures are precluded from the analysis. Over 90 percent of the territories exchanged in this subset of cases were directly contiguous to both the gaining and losing sides. Although this demonstrates that almost all of the territories in interstate exchanges are important in one way to the parties, there is not enough variation to help us explain when military conflict will result and when the transfer will be peaceful. Thus, we are left with only one indicator of territorial importance, the size of the area exchanged (as in the previous chapter, we use the log value of area in order to mitigate the statistical effects of extreme values).

EXPANSIONIST PRESSURES

The limitations imposed by this subset of cases were considerably less in measuring the other variables. The propensity for territorial expansion is measured with three separate variables. We look first at the change in a state's total population over the twenty years prior to the territorial exchange in order to measure population pressures for expansion. The greater the increase in population, we hypothesize, the more pressure for territorial expansion and the greater the likelihood for military conflict to be a part of that expansion. To measure economic pressures, we focus on the change in industrial capabilities over the ten years prior to the exchange. Here, the industrial capabilities are indicated by the average of a state's iron/steel production and its energy consumption.[17] The assumption is that the greater the economic growth, the higher the propensity for territorial expansion in a violent fashion. It might be noted that these two indicators represent separate sources of expansionist pressure. The population and economic pressure variables are virtually uncorrelated; Pearson's correlations are .10 and .01 for the losing and gaining side respectively, with neither coefficient statistically significant.

The two previous indicators refer to pressures for potential territorial expansion. In order to gain a sense of the actual expansionist tendencies of a state, we also include a third variable: the net gain or loss in territory for each side over the twenty years prior to the territorial exchange. Choucri and North employ a similar measure (total colonial area) to capture their notion of lateral pressure.[18] Prior, extensive acquisition of territory by the gaining side in the territorial exchange would seem to predict a strong desire for expansion and perhaps a willingness to use military force in pursuit of that end. Correspondingly, recent expansion by the losing side would seem to indicate a willingness to resist with force any losses in territorial control.

RELATIVE CAPABILITY

Finally, the relative capability distribution between the gaining and losing sides is indicated by the ratio of their industrial capabilities at the time of the exchange. The reader will recall that industrial capabilities are indicated by iron/steel production and energy consumption. A ratio of greater than one indicates that the gaining side in the exchange has more capability than the losing side, and we hypothesize that military conflict is therefore more likely. It may seem surprising to some that our measure of national capabilities does not include a military component. Measures of military capability (personnel and expenditures) are highly correlated (Pearson's $r=.75$) with the industrial capabilities indicators, and the inclusion of the military indicators did not significantly affect the results reported below. For the sake of parsimony, then, we did not include those military indicators in our capability measure.

METHOD OF ANALYSIS

Also in chapter 3, we used LISREL analysis to combine multiple dimensions of the same latent variable and assess the variable's effect on the likelihood of military conflict. In this subset of cases, a different method of analysis is required. There are only single indicators for the variables of territorial importance and relative capability, eliminating the need for a technique to combine dimensions into an integrated variable. Expansionist pressure for each side is measured with three separate indicators. Yet, as noted above, the population and economic pressure indicators are separate aspects of expansionist pressure and therefore cannot be integrated from a conceptual vantage point (or a statistical one as factor analysis requires indicators to be correlated with each other in order to "load" on the latent variable). The same can be said for combining either of those indicators of potential expansion with the indicator of prior territorial expansion. Each indicator must be considered separately, and we expect that the strength of the relationship to military conflict will vary according to each indicator.

Table 4.3 Summary of Variables and Indicators

Variable	Operational Measure
Importance	Size of area exchanged in square kilometers
Relative Capabilities	Average of the ratio of the gaining side's iron/steel production and energy consumption, respectively, to those of the losing side
Population Pressures	Change in total population from $t-20$ to t
Economic Pressures	Average change in iron/steel production and energy consumption from $t-10$ to t
Prior Territorial Expansion	Net gain or loss in territory from $t-20$ to t

When considering predictor variables (territorial importance, relative capabilities, population pressures, economic pressures, and prior territorial expansion) of a dichotomous independent variable (military conflict), the appropriate technique is logistic regression.[19] Logistic regression is similar to ordinary least squares (OLS) linear regression in that the results provide coefficient estimates, significance tests, and estimates of the model's overall fit with the data. Yet, logistic regression takes into account that the outcome variable (military conflict) can only take on two different values (the presence or absence of military conflict). In the next section, we use logistic regression to ascertain how well the variables we have identified explain which interstate territorial changes will involve military conflict and which will be completed peacefully.

A summary of the indicators used to measure each variable is given in Table 4.3.

Empirical Results

In our model, we had assumed a symmetry in the effect that the expansionist pressures of the gaining and losing side had on the likelihood of military conflict; that is, we reasoned that pressures on both sides were significant and equally important. Empirically, however, there emerged clear, systematic differences in the effects of the two sides' characteristics. Specifically, in the period prior to 1914, it is the expansionist pressures of the losing side that are related to military conflict. In contrast, the gaining sides' expansionist tendencies are the only ones significant after the outbreak of World War I. The relationships between the other two variables (territorial importance and relative capabilities) also varied systematically according to these time frames. Thus, we report two sets of results below: one for the first time period (prior to 1914) and including the expansionist pressure variables for the losing side of the exchange and one for the second period (after 1914) that includes the expansion pressure variables for the gaining side. Possible reasons for these temporal differences, as well as a discussion of the results, are covered in the concluding section of this chapter.

PRE-1914 PERIOD

Table 4.4 gives the results of the analysis for the pre-World War I period. Once again, only the expansion pressure variables for the losing side are included (the territorial, population, and economic expansion indicators for the gaining side are not included; their inclusion does not significantly improve the fit of the model nor is the significance or direction of the results reported in Table 4.4 substantially different).

The overall fit of the model can be evaluated by several measures. First, there is the logit equivalent of the regression R^2, which in this case has a value of .35. This result and the finding that two of the five predictor variables are not statistically significant indicate that the model only fits moderately well for this period. This conclusion is confirmed by looking at another measure of overall fit, Somer's DXY (this is a measure of two-way association varying between 0 and 1); the value here is .57, again indicating a moderate degree of success for the model. Overall, the model predicts military conflict or its absence correctly about 71 percent of the time, with about the same error rate (false-positives and false-negatives) for predicting conflict-ridden and peaceful transfers of territory.

Table 4.4 Interstate Territorial Changes and Military Conflict, 1816 to 1913

	Logistic Regression	
Variable	Coefficient (standard error)	Significance
Intercept	−4.04 (1.95)	.04
Population Pressures	−3.50 (1.66)	.04
Economic Pressures	−65.14 (23.75)	.01
Prior Territorial Expansion	−.13 (.28)	.63
Relative Capabilities	.40 (.18)	.03
Territorial Importance	−.10 (.10)	.30

Equivalent R^2 = .35
Somer's DYX = .57
Correct Prediction Rate = 70.7%
False Positive Rate = 28.6%
False Negative Rate = 29.7%

We now turn to the individual variables, focusing on their

coefficients and whether we can say that they have a statistically significant effect on the likelihood of military conflict. The importance of the territory is apparently unrelated to whether or not the territorial exchange will be a violent one. Prior to World War I, states fought over territory that was expansive as often as they tangled over small pieces of land; territorial importance, as measured here, was not related to military conflict. More significant are the variables related to the relative capabilities of the two sides and the expansionist pressures on the losing side. As predicted, military conflict is associated with the gaining side being more powerful. This is consistent with the notion that larger states take advantage of capability differences for territorial aggrandizement.

With respect to the expansion variables, surprisingly, military conflict is associated with a relative *decline* in population and economic growth. This suggests that as a state loses status, it is vulnerable to raids on its homeland. Previous territorial expansion on the part of the losing side is unrelated to the outbreak of military conflict. This means that conflict is not affected by whether the losing side has recently acquired or lost portions of its territory. In summary, for the period prior to World War I, more powerful states took advantage of declining states in order to seize vulnerable territories. In other instances of territorial transfer, the conditions were more favorable to a peaceful transfer.

POST-1914 PERIOD

In the period after 1914, the expansionist tendencies of the gaining side seem to enhance the chances for military conflict; the results for this period are presented in Table 4.5. In terms of overall performance of the model, the results are not overwhelming. The equivalent R^2 value is .29 and Somer's DXY is .56. The model can correctly predict three-fourths of the outcomes, but there still are a significant number of false alarms and miss fires.

Both the territorial expansion and the population growth variables (for the gaining side) are statistically significant in the expected direction. This means that a state with a history of expansionism and population pressures pushing it outward is likely to use military force to seize territory from its neighbors. Importantly, the expansion outward is apparently not driven by economic pressures. These results can, in part, lend some credibility to the power transition hypothesis.[20] The dynamic of change in the gaining side is a significant source of conflict, although conflict occurs at a variety of capability distributions among many different kinds of states, not only at approximate parity between major powers as the power transition hypothesis suggests.

Table 4.5 Interstate Territorial Changes and Military Conflict, 1914 to 1980

Variable	Logistic Regression Coefficient (standard error)	Significance
Intercept	.22 (.87)	.80
Population Pressures	2.07 (.87)	.02
Economic Pressures	-4.77 (5.81)	.41
Prior Territorial Expansion	.58 (.29)	.04
Relative Capabilities	.02 (.03)	.41
Territorial Importance	.12 (.06)	.05

Equivalent R^2 = .29
Somer's DYX = .56
Correct Prediction Rate = 74.5%
False Positive Rate = 25.0%
False Negative Rate = 25.7%

The findings for the relative capability and territorial importance variables are almost the opposite of the patterns noted for the pre-1914 period. Preponderance by the gaining side is no longer necessarily a precursor to the seizure of territory with military force. States may fight over territory even if they are approximately equal in capability and sometimes even the stronger side loses territory to its weaker rival. Yet, the post-1914 period also sees states prone to fight over large territories, with the territorial importance variable being a statistically significant predictor of military conflict. In summary, military conflict in this period is driven by internal expansion pressures in the gaining state, resulting in violence over areas viewed as important.

In the next section, we discuss the coherence and limitations of these results, and offer some theoretical explanations.

Conclusion

The overall results of our analysis, while not dramatic, are coherent. Expansion on the part of the gaining side is related to military conflict in the period after 1914, while decline on the part of the losing side is related to violent change in the earlier period. In the earlier era, the stronger gaining side seemed to prey on the decline of the losing state and seize new territory through the use of military force. After 1914, preponderance was apparently not much of a factor. Rather, states fought over territory they regarded as important. In general, the model provides some important clues as to when states will fight over territory, but the modest results suggest that the specification of relevant variables or their measurement requires some improvement.

Beyond the inadequacy of the model to predict all the cases of military conflict, there is the seemingly puzzling finding of different patterns of conflict for the pre- and post-World War I periods. Yet, one might generally expect that relationships will vary across time and space, and monumental events such as a world war can be key transition points in changing relationships.[21] Furthermore, Singer, Bremer, and Stuckey have noted important theoretical and empirical differences between the time periods identified here.[22] An examination of the two periods reveals some possible reasons for their differences.

Prior to 1914, and with a few exceptions, the leading states in the international system were successful at managing challenges to the established order. Attempts at expansion by a member of the "club" or land grabs by emerging states were generally put down. The Concert of Europe was committed to the status quo and this included the maintenance of state boundaries in Europe. Acquisition of homeland territory through the use of military force generally took place at the periphery of the system, such as occurred in the War of the Pacific between Bolivia and Chile. Territorial wars resulting in an alteration of state boundaries were opportunistic, a chance to expand one's borders into a disputed adjacent area. This opportunity was made possible by a capability advantage and the waning influence of a sovereign in the region or international system. This is largely consistent with Zuk's findings that the relative capability distribution, not merely the growth of a state, exercised a great impact on territorial expansion and the likelihood of military conflict prior to World War I.[23]

The acquisition of territory in the pre-1914 period also was much less of the zero-sum game it would become later on. States experiencing expansionist pressures could settle new colonial territories, as most of the major powers did in Africa and Asia. Note that Choucri and North found a positive relationship between lateral pressure and *colonial* expansion. The ability to acquire expansive colonial areas to relieve internal pressures may account for the insignificance of those pressures in predicting conflict over homeland territory. It may also account for the failure of the territorial importance variable, measured by the size of the area, to be significant; if land is not a scarce commodity, the size of an area alone will not be a very good indicator of a land's importance.

Although our model successfully predicted almost three-fourths of the cases of military conflict, there is a notable pattern among the failed predictions. Most of the failures were those involving the decline of the Ottoman Empire. This may at first appear odd in that the Ottoman Empire was a classic case of a declining power in the nineteenth century; our model suggests that it was exactly this kind of state that was most vulnerable to losing territory through military force. Yet, contrary to the specifications of our model, the Ottoman Empire did not always lose territory to more powerful states; indeed, it lost territory to comparable or even weaker states. Nevertheless, even though the gaining side was weak, the exchange was facilitated under the auspices of the major powers, consistent with our basic findings.

World War I signalled some important changes in the international system. The Concert of Europe had disintegrated and so had the coordination of the major powers which managed change between themselves and other states in an international system that had been Eurocentric. Unlike the previous era, the expansionist tendencies of some states (for example, Japan and Germany) were no longer restrained by the international community; not surprisingly then, expansion on the part of the gaining side becomes associated with territorial acquisition through the use of military force. Furthermore, most of the world's land had been charted by the early part of the twentieth century. This meant that any territorial expansion now had to come at the expense of some other state, and with the decline of colonial territory, at the expense of some other state's homeland. With land a more scarce resource, states began to fight over those areas that were considered important; large areas could no longer be gained or replaced by easy expansion into dependent territories. Consequently, territorial importance emerges as an important predictor of military conflict.

Study of individual cases of territorial change and military conflict after World War I finds our model particularly inadequate in predicting war and seizure of territory in the Middle East. Part of this difficulty lies in our limited measure of territorial importance—the size of the area. Although territories such as the West Bank and the Golan Heights are relatively small in size, they are not small compared to the size of Israel. Furthermore, both are important strategically to the defense of the Israeli state; these aspects are not captured by our measure of importance, but do suggest that we are correct to focus on the importance concept in understanding the conditions for military conflict. Thus, we might suggest that the failed prediction is in part the result of our indicator, the theoretical notions seem validated. In addition, Israel was a dynamic and growing state both demographically and economically, which accords with our other results.

The other cases in which the model fails are those exchanges following World War II. Many of these exchanges involved the return of territory seized during the 1930s by the aggressors in World War II. In other cases, the territory exchanged was compensation (in the form of favorable border adjustments) given to the winners of the war and their allies by the defeated powers Italy, Germany, and Japan. These may represent a subset of cases largely unrelated to the acquisition of large areas by expansionist states typical of the other cases in this era. Instead, they represent territorial adjustments that are a function of the outcome of war, and therefore not explained by our model which focuses on expansion pressures and territorial importance as sources of conflict.

Overall, realpolitik explanations of international behavior are better supported in this set of cases than in those the previous chapter. In each of the two eras, expansion (or decline) factors were significant in affecting the chances for military conflict. Furthermore, territorial importance was only significant in the second period. It may be that power politics concerns are more relevant in state-to-state interactions and when the stakes are considered high (note that to some degree all the territories exchanged in this subset of cases were valuable as they were homeland territories). Furthermore, unlike national independence, few if any international norms exist regarding the exchange of homeland territory. Consequently, there are not strong international restraints against the pursuit of power and territory in these cases.

Nevertheless, even at their strongest, the realpolitik factors failed to predict over one-fourth of the instances of military conflict. In addition, the relative capabilities factor lost its significance after World War I; factors internal to the state and territorial importance were more related to the use of military force. Combined with the problems cited with the measurement of territorial importance, this suggests that claims of the exclusivity, or even primacy, of realpolitik explanations of international behavior are dubious.

The transfer of territory, through peaceful means or otherwise, does not signal the end of claims over the territory involved, nor does it necessarily mean that conflict between the two parties to the exchange is over. We have already looked at conditions for military conflict in the birth of a state and in this chapter we have focused on when states will fight over territorial transfers. In chapter 5, we turn our attention to the relationship between those territorial changes and future relations between the parties to the exchange.

Notes

1. Mostafa Rejai and Cynthia Enloe, "Nation-States and State-Nations" in *Perspectives on World Politics*, eds. Michael Smith, Richard Little, and Michael Shackleton (Chatham, N.J.: Chatham House, 1981), 37–46.
2. See James Dunnigan and Austin Bay, *A Quick and Dirty Guide to War* (New York: William Morrow, 1986).
3. For a list of major powers and their dates of inclusion, see Melvin Small and J. David Singer, *Resort to Arms* (Beverly Hills: Sage Publications, 1982), 47–50.
4. Unlike previous figures, Figure 4.1 uses ten-year intervals, instead of five-year blocks, to chart the frequency of military conflict over time. This was done because the relatively few cases in some time periods gave

a distorted view of the overall propensity for violence in a given era. The ten-year interval smooths out some of those aberrations.

5. Nazli Choucri and Robert North, *Nations in Conflict* (San Francisco: Freeman, 1975).
6. Our analysis has a number of differences from that of Choucri and North. Our conceptualization does not include military expansion pressures nor do we treat the expansion pressures as interrelated and mutually supporting. In fact, we find empirical support for the idea that economic and demographic pressures are by and large empirically distinct. Finally, we do not confine our analysis to only the major powers nor to the 1870–1914 period.
7. For an argument on how population pressures may *lessen* the likelihood of war, see Julian Simon, "Lebensraum: Paradoxically, Population Growth May Eventually End Wars," *Journal of Conflict Resolution* 33 (1989):164–180.
8. We do acknowledge that conceptually it is conceivable that economic pressures can stem from demographic pressures. The drive for new markets or resources, for example, may be a function of increasing population. Yet, as we note above, these were separate dimensions of expansion in reality.
9. Howard Koch, Robert North, and Dina Zinnes, "Some Theoretical Notes on Geography and International Conflict," *Journal of Conflict Resolution* 4 (1960):4–14.
10. V.I. Lenin, *Imperialism: The Highest Stage of Capitalism* (New York: International Publishers, 1939). In contrast, Tony Smith argues that British imperialism in the nineteenth century was characterized by opposition to territorial annexation and support of *open door* policies. The motivation was similar to that of territorial expansion (that is, economic benefit through trade), but the means were quite different; British policy toward China was the most notable example; see Tony Smith, *The Pattern of Imperialism: The United States, Great Britain, and the Late-Industrializing World Since 1815* (Cambridge: Cambridge University Press, 1981), 15–49.
11. Gary Zuk, "National Growth and International Conflict: A Reexamination of the Choucri and North Thesis," *Journal of Politics* 47 (1985):269–281.
12. J.R.V. Prescott, *The Geography of Frontiers and Boundaries*. (Chicago: Aldine Publishing, 1965), 114.
13. Robert Mandel, "Roots of Modern Interstate Border Disputes," *Journal of Conflict Resolution* 24 (1980):427–454.
14. Implied in J.R.V. Prescott, *Political Geography* (London: Methuen and Co., 1972).
15. Randolph Siverson and Michael Sullivan, "The Distribution of Power and the Onset of War," *Journal of Conflict Resolution* 27 (1983):473–494.
16. John Vasquez, "Capability, Types of War, Peace," *Western Political Quarterly* 38 (1986):313–327. See also chapter 6 of Benjamin Most and Harvey Starr, *Inquiry, Logic, and International Politics* (Columbia: University of South Carolina Press, 1989).
17. When a territorial transfer occurs less than 10 or 20 years after the state enters the international system, we look at population and economic growth in the time since the system entry. In a few cases, the territorial transfer occurs in the year following the system entry and therefore, population and

economic growth are recorded as zero. When the 10- or 20-year period overlapped with World War years (which are coded as *missing data* by the Correlates of War Project), we used data from the years prior to the war. All data are taken from the Correlates of War Project.
18. Choucri and North, *Nations in Conflict.*
19. See John Aldrich and Forrest Nelson, "Linear Probability, Logit, and Probit Models" (Sage University Paper Series on Quantitative Applications in the Social Sciences, 07-045. Beverly Hills: Sage Publications, 1984).
20. A.F.K. Organski, *World Politics,* 2nd ed. (New York: Alfred Knopf, 1968).
21. Most and Starr, *Inquiry, Logic, and International Politics.*
22. J. David Singer, Stuart Bremer, and John Stuckey, "Capability Distribution, Uncertainty, and Major Power War, 1820–1965" in *Peace, War, and Numbers* ed. Bruce Russett (Beverly Hills: Sage Publications, 1972), 19–48.
23. Zuk, "National Growth."

CHAPTER 5

Territorial Changes and Recurring Conflict

"The history of war and peace is largely identical with the history of territorial changes as results of war and causes of the next war."
—Erich Weede

We have noted in previous chapters that some states must fight to gain their independence and then fight again to acquire new areas or to hold onto existing territorial possessions. Even after a territorial change occurs, however, the basis for dispute between the gaining and losing states does not necessarily terminate. Sometimes, a territorial change initiates a recurring cycle of violence between the same pair of states. The division of India and Pakistan in 1947 sets the stage for two more wars in the next quarter century. Similarly, conflict in the Middle East has not dissipated (some would say it has intensified) by changes in territorial boundaries by the principal protagonists. Yet, in other cases, a territorial change has ushered in a relatively peaceful era of relations between states. The purchase of Louisiana from the French in the early nineteenth century was followed by years of amicable Franco-American relations.

This chapter completes the investigation of the sequence of relationships between territorial changes and militarized conflict. In earlier chapters, we discussed when military conflict is a part of the process of national independence and when it is involved in exchanges of homeland territory between established states. Now we are concerned with how the territorial changes themselves have an influence on the chances for future conflict between those same states. In a sense, we have come full circle from using territorial changes as units of analysis to employing them as an explanatory variable. Our goal in this chapter is to understand why military conflict occurs (and reoccurs) in some instances between states that were a party to a territorial exchange, while conflict abates or ends in other cases.

Understanding recurring conflict has a number of theoretical and policy benefits. We have noted that a common form of conflict involves continuing rivalries between the same sets of states over time. This suggests that individual conflicts are not independent events as most studies of international relations implicitly treat them.[1] Therefore, we need a greater understanding of how conflict events are related to each other. We believe that looking at the impact of territorial changes on subsequent conflict contributes to that understanding. In addition, the consequences of repeated conflict are profound from both a theoretical and policy viewpoint. Leng found that states generally adopt more coercive bargaining strategies in successive disputes with the same enemy, and the result was almost always war by the third confrontation.[2] This highlights the importance of settling territorial transfers properly at the initial stage, lest lingering tensions escalate at a later time.

From a decision-makers perspective, one would want to complete a territorial transfer under the most favorable conditions or terms possible. Yet, a long-term concern must be how stable that transfer will be and what are the consequences attached to those terms or conditions. Many current conflicts trace their origins to the narrow, short-term decisions of states. The Israeli occupation of the Golan Heights and the West Bank as a result of the Six Day War in 1967 obviously yielded some strategic, political, and psychological benefits that country. Nevertheless, the control over those areas has brought only a small measure of long-term peace and security to Israel; it has fought two subsequent wars with its neighbors and endured numerous terrorist attacks as a consequence of the unresolved Palestinian question and the occupation of those lands. In contrast, Israel's decision to give back the Sinai Peninsula to Egypt as a part of the Camp David Accords has mitigated verbal conflict between the two antagonists and has thus far ended military conflict between them.

Dissatisfaction with the outcome, as we discuss below, is not the only reason to expect future military conflict from changes in boundaries. Japan has consistently objected to the Soviet occupation of the Kuril Islands, but there is no indication that a military confrontation between the two states is likely any time soon. Bolivia still maintains some enmity toward Chile for the loss of territory during the War of the Pacific over a hundred years ago; yet, in that case also, armed conflict has been, and is likely to continue to be, avoided.

By understanding the conditions for recurring conflict from territorial changes, decision-makers might first try to manipulate those conditions so that future conflict might be avoided or mitigated. Of course, some of those conditions may not be subject to any manipulation (for example, the intrinsic importance of the territory) or only limited influence (such as the power distribution between the states) by decision-makers. In those instances, there is at minimum an enhanced ability to anticipate future problems and perhaps deal with them by reference to appropriate actions in pursuit of the peaceful resolution of disputes.

In the next section, we explore how common the phenomenon of recurring conflict after territorial changes really is, with appropriate consideration of regional and temporal differences.

Empirical Patterns

Pierre Allan's notion of diplomatic time captures to some degree the extent to which prior events influence later actions.[3] The assumption in Allan's model is that such influence dissipates as the prior event becomes more distant from the time at hand. This assumption is based on psychological models of memory loss, in which people's short-term memory is thought to undergo an exponential decay.[4] If extrapolated to state behavior, it would be expected that prior events will decrease in their impact on state decisions. For example, the Iran hostage crisis had a greater impact on United States policy in the early 1980s than it will in the 1990s. In the context of this study, a territorial change is thought to exercise a declining impact over time on the chances for conflict between the gaining and losing sides in the exchange.

To determine if territorial changes have any relationship to later conflict, we first examine how frequently parties to a territorial change engage in future military conflict with each other. We focus on all cases of territorial changes involving states as the gaining and losing sides; these include the cases studied in chapters 3 and 4 as well as exchanges of colonial territory between states.[5] In total, we look at 415 territorial changes. In making an assessment of future conflict, we are confronted with the problems of how to define military conflict and what time frame following the territorial change is appropriate. In order to identify subsequent serious conflict between the parties to the territorial change, we focus on the occurrence of "militarized disputes" between them. A militarized dispute is a "set of interactions between or among states involving threats to use military force, displays of military force, or actual uses of military force . . . these acts must be explicit, overt, nonaccidental, and government sanctioned."[6] Such disputes include a range of serious conflict including confrontations, crises, and full-scale wars. The common element is that the disagreements are serious enough to warrant the threat or use of military force.

Because states are involved in many ways in militarized disputes, we restrict our analyses to two dispute configurations. The first is when the territorial change parties are the primary initiator and primary target in the dispute (that is, they are the initial and primary actors). The other occurs when one of the parties is either the primary initiator or target and its opponent is a secondary party on the other side. Thus, we ignore militarized disputes in which both territorial change parties had only a secondary role in the conflict or those disputes in which the parties were on the same side.

Having decided to focus on militarized disputes between the participants, we turn next to determining an appropriate time frame after the territorial change to look for the incidence of those disputes. As indicated above, territorial changes should have a decreasing effect over time on the incidence of conflict between the same parties to the exchange. Thus, it would be inappropriate, for example, to look for the occurrence of a dispute between two states in 1935 which had completed a territorial exchange 100 years earlier. To investigate this, we decided to consider whether the parties to the exchange had experienced a militarized dispute at intervals of 5, 10, 20, and 30 years after the exchange. Militarized disputes, because they represent serious and dangerous actions, are relatively infrequent occurrences. Thus, the five-year time frame allows us a reasonable amount of time to see the immediate effects of the territorial change.

At the other extreme, some territorial disputes have long-standing histories and it may be many years before such animosities are manifested in a militarized dispute. We choose the 30-year time frame because it roughly represents one generation of leadership; beyond this time, the connection between any conflict and a territorial change becomes more tenuous. One problem with the 30-year time frame is that those changes after 1950 have not had a full 30 years in our data set (which only includes disputes up until 1980). Thus, the figures for 30 years may be somewhat underestimated.[7]

Figure 5.1 shows the percentage of territorial changes that were followed by a militarized dispute between the same parties 5, 10, 20, and 30 years after the exchange. After 5 years, approximately 20 percent of the parties to a territorial exchange have faced each other in a militarized dispute. This is significantly greater than would be predicted by chance (that is, the likelihood that any two states in the international system would be involved in a militarized dispute against each other). The percentage of territorial changes that are followed by future disputes increases over time, although the further one moves from the original territorial exchange, the more the rate of increase in the territorial changes that join the list of those that experience subsequent military conflict declines. One generation after the exchange, almost 40 percent of the territorial changes have been followed by a militarized dispute between the same parties.

Table 5.1 Regional Distribution of Recurring Conflict

Region	Total Changes	Percent Future Conflict (N)	Disputes per Change (N)
Americas	61	36.1 (22)	1.28 (78)
Europe	103	63.1 (65)	1.65 (170)
Africa	90	28.9 (26)	.89 (80)
Middle East	69	47.8 (33)	1.49 (103)
Asia	92	31.5 (29)	1.40 (129)
Total	415	42.2 (175)	1.35 (560)

Figure 5.1 Amount of Future Conflict

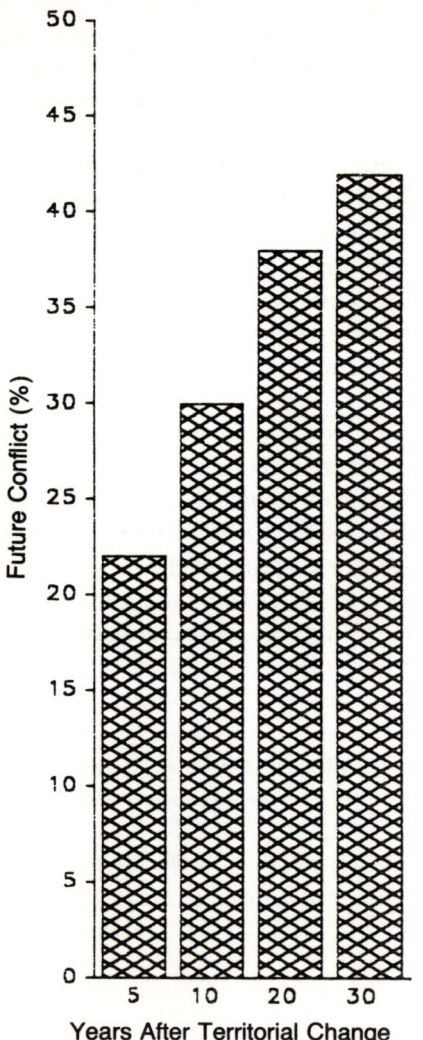

Throughout the book, we have considered regional differences in territorial changes. Many of these differences can be accounted for by the models we have developed, while other patterns are rooted in the unique historical development of each region. Regional differences are also evident in the frequency of future conflict. Table 5.1 reveals the percentage of territorial changes in each region that experienced at least one militarized dispute within 30 years after the exchange. The table also reports how many total disputes (as many territorial changes were followed by more than one dispute between the same parties) occurred after the territorial changes in the region; the aggregate total is reported as well as a calculation of the average number of disputes per territorial change.

Once again, the regions with the densest collection of states are the ones with the greatest percentage of future conflict: Europe and the Middle East. In each case, almost 50 percent or more of the territorial changes would see the same two parties clash in a future militarized dispute. Despite the greater frequency of military conflict in these regions, the other three regions have had their share of recurring conflict with at least one-fourth of the exchange cases followed by conflict. Looking at the total number of future disputes reveals that, ceteris paribus, one can expect that every instance of territorial change between two states will result in, on the average, slightly more than one militarized dispute between the parties. There is not much regional variation on this dimension except in Africa, perhaps because in many cases of territorial change states were becoming independent and subsequent relations between the new state and the former imperial/colonial power have been amicable. The primary regional differences are evident when looking across centuries. Table 5.2 provides this breakdown.

From a general perspective, nineteenth century territorial changes seem more likely to prompt future conflict than those in the next century; 59.8 percent involved future disputes in the nineteenth century, while only 36.8 percent did so in the twentieth century. The same pattern is evident for the average number of militarized disputes per territorial change; the figures are 1.90 per territorial change in the first period and 1.18 for the second period. Yet one must recall that many of the territorial changes in the twentieth century have not experienced a full 30 years following the exchange, and thus the figures for the twentieth century may be underestimated.

Table 5.2 Regional Distribution of Recurring Conflict, by Century

Region	Total Changes	Percent Future Conflict (N)	Disputes per Change (N)
19th Century			
Americas	27	63.0 (17)	2.48 (67)
Europe	26	61.5 (16)	1.69 (44)
Africa	17	52.9 (9)	1.41 (24)
Middle East	9	55.6 (5)	1.89 (17)
Asia	18	61.1 (11)	1.78 (32)
Total	97	59.8 (58)	1.90 (184)
20th Century			
Americas	34	14.7 (5)	.32 (11)
Europe	77	63.6 (49)	1.64 (126)
Africa	73	23.2 (17)	.77 (56)
Middle East	60	46.7 (28)	1.43 (86)
Asia	74	24.3 (18)	1.31 (97)
Total	318	36.8 (117)	1.18 (376)

Nevertheless, the intercentury differences are striking on a regional level. Future disputes after a territorial change in the Western Hemisphere are almost eight times more likely in the nineteenth century than in the twentieth century. Perhaps some of this difference can be attributed to the emergence of the United States as a policeman in the region and the success of the Organization of American States in mediating disputes. Whereas an average territorial change produced over two disputes in the nineteenth century, that number has declined to the point where there is only one dispute per every three exchanges in the twentieth century. Africa also shows a significant decline in the likelihood and number of militarized disputes from territorial changes. As noted above, this may be the result of the predominance of independence cases (and increasingly peaceful ones) in the twentieth century as compared to battles between imperial/colonial powers over African territory in the nineteenth century.

Table 5.3 States Most Involved in Recurring Conflict

Year of Change	Number of States Involved	Number of Disputes
1949	India–Pakistan	15
1949	Egypt–Israel	11
1958	India–Pakistan	10
1853	United States–Mexico	8
1848	United States–Mexico	8
1905	Russia–China	7
1900	Russia–China	7
1967	Israel–Syria	7
1949	Israel–Jordan	7
1911	Germany–France	7
1919	Belgium–Germany	7
1898	Russia–China	7
1878	United Kingdom–Ottoman Empire	7
1842	United Kingdom–United States	7
1905	Japan–Russia	6
1919	Italy–France	6
1919	France–Germany	6
1846	United Kingdom–United States	6

Beyond regional concerns of where recurring conflict is taking place, we are also concerned with which territorial changes have been most susceptible to repeated conflict. The territorial changes that have experienced the most future conflict are listed in Table 5.3. Despite 40 years and 15 militarized disputes (including several wars), India and Pakistan's dispute over Kashmir has continued to fester since the original division of territory in 1949. Closely behind are the territorial changes involving the creation of the Israeli state in 1949 and its expansion in 1967. Several cases on the list indicate that boundary disputes and demarcations set off a series of continuing disputes, such as those between the United States and Britain over the American-Canadian border. This list also demonstrates that controversies over Cyprus have a long history as the exchange between Britain and the Ottoman Empire was only beginning with the exchange of that island territory. Finally, the number of disputes following the French seizure of German territory after World War I is only another piece of evidence of how the postwar settlement failed to bring peace to Europe.

There is considerable variation in the frequency and magnitude of military conflict following the exchange of territory between two states. In the following section, we identify several conditions that may account for why some territorial changes usher in an era of peace, while others seem only to begin or continue a cycle of conflict between states.

The Conditions for Military Conflict

Among the consistent themes in this book is that the importance of a territory conditions the behaviour of states. In this chapter, we again rely on the importance of a territory to help distinguish between territorial changes that result in further military conflict and those that promote peaceful relations. We also look again to power distribution factors to explain the conditions under which one of the parties to the original territorial change might clash with the other party. Yet, beyond these conditions, which formed the basis of much of the analysis in previous chapters, we focus on a third condition—the perceived legitimacy of the original territorial change. Thus, importance, the power distribution, and legitimacy form the components of our model of recurring conflict; the logic for the inclusion of each factor is discussed below.

After a territory comes under the jurisdiction of another state, its intrinsic or relational importance does not change dramatically. The physical size of the territory is, of course, virtually immutable. The human capital and natural resources within the boundaries of the territory can change, but usually not significantly in the period immediately following the transfer of sovereignty (with a few exceptions, resource rich, sparsely populated areas do not suddenly become densely populated—through migration or increase in the birth rate—nor do resources become depleted in a short period of time). Similarly, the geographic location of the territory, which in part influences its strategic and psychological importance, also is the same as it was at the time of the territorial change.

Our argument is that if the territory was viewed as important at the time of the territorial change, it is likely still to be considered important and this may be a condition that makes the parties to the exchange more willing to fight, particularly the losing side. The yielding side in the territorial exchange is likely to be more resentful over the loss of territory if that territory is valuable (note the difference in reaction when people lose a nickel versus when they lose 500 dollars). Such resentment may breed attempts to reacquire the territory (note that Egypt's attack against Israel in the Yom Kippur War was in part to get back the Sinai Peninsula) or it may plant a poisoned seed in its relationship with the gaining side that may prompt future conflict between the two sides which on the surface may be over apparently unrelated matters (American conflicts with Mexico in the mid-nineteenth century fit this pattern). Thus, we anticipate that territorial importance will be a good predictor of future conflict.

When a state relinquishes valuable territory, it may not feel any resentment toward the gaining state if the transaction is perceived to be a fair one. The sale of territory, for example, may involve a very valuable land area, but such a transfer is usually a voluntary arrangement with appropriate compensation paid to the seller. In that circumstance, the resentment that can breed future conflict is not likely to occur. Thus, we are concerned with the legitimacy, or perceived propriety, of the transaction. Fairness is a difficult concept to measure, and objective assessments are problematic in most situations. Nevertheless, it seems plausible that if the losing side felt cheated out of the territory in some way, it would be less hesitant to threaten or use military force against the other party in the future. In particular, the losing side may feel no obligation to abide by the outcome of the territorial exchange if it is regarded as illegitimate, or if the loser believes that—tit for tat—it is entitled to something in return for the injustice. Thus, we expect that the less the perceived legitimacy of the original territorial exchange, the greater the likelihood that the two sides will meet later in a militarized dispute.

Finally, we recognize that an important territory transferred illegitimately may increase the willingness of a state to threaten or use military force, but such conditions say little about the opportunity or ability to take such action. Thus, it is necessary to add relative capabilities to our model. The losing state might only violently express its resentment against the other party to the territorial exchange if the loser feels it can win the next interaction. If the capability differential is too great, the losing side may not judge its chances as good enough to provoke a confrontation with an opponent. Thus, a capability advantage that favors the gaining side from the previous territorial exchange is hypothesized to be the least likely for future military conflict, with the likelihood increasing as the losing side increases its power relative to the gaining side.

Our argument is that future conflict is likely when the territorial change involved important territory and the method of transition was perceived as illegitimate by a losing side that has the capability to redress grievances. In the context of understanding future conflict, in the next section we attempt to describe what would make a territory important and the transaction illegitimate by discussing these concerns jointly with our operational measures of amorphous concepts.

Measurement Models

IMPORTANCE

Again, we use the size of the area and the population of the territory at the time of the exchange to represent the intrinsic importance of the territory. The first indicator of relational importance is the geographic proximity of the territory to the gaining and losing sides. Territory will be considered more significant to the parties if it was geographically proximate. Thus we code the geographic location of the territory exchanged on an ordinal scale as contiguous and noncontiguous. Contiguity is defined as the territory sharing a direct land border with the party in question or separated by a body of water not exceeding 150 statute miles (240 kilometers) in width.[8] Relational importance is considered separately for the gaining and losing side. The relative importance of the territory to each side will vary and in this case there is no reason to expect that the indicators for each side will be correlated.

Although proximity is a key aspect of relational importance, it does not capture all the aspects of importance attached to territory by a state. Thus, we also consider whether the territory exchanged was formerly the homeland territory of the losing state or whether it was colonial or some other kind of dependent territory. A similar determination is made for the gaining side. A state losing homeland territory will, in our view, be more resentful as its former citizens have been incorporated into another state and the territorial exchange results in a net loss in the size of the state. Conversely, the attachment to a dependent territory may be primarily economic, and its loss does not generate the nationalistic feelings that homeland territory does. The gaining side will also regard the territory as more important if the new area becomes part of its homeland instead of another territorial possession to manage and exploit economically.

Homeland territory in a territorial exchange is almost always geographically proximate to one or both sides, but proximity alone cannot indicate the distinction in significance between homeland and dependent territory. Thus, we use two ordinal indicators to measure the relational importance of a territory: the presence or absence of contiguity and whether the territory was (or is in the case of the gaining side) homeland territory. Separate variables based on these indicators are constructed for the gaining and losing sides in the exchange.

LEGITIMACY

The legitimacy of a territorial exchange is a difficult concept to measure. In social contract theory, people join society of their own free will; an order established otherwise is regarded as illegitimate. Applying this to territorial changes, we might expect transfers from one sovereign jurisdiction to another to be regarded as legitimate if the population affected approved of such a change. In the modern world, people do not form societies as they might have in a state of nature. They are occasionally asked, however, to express their preferences in the form of a plebiscite. A plebiscite approving the territorial change suggests that indigenous groups may be less likely to seek relief from their former government; thus, tension-generating claims, arising out of ethnic or political concerns, between the parties to the exchange might be less likely.

There are several problems with looking at plebiscites to indicate legitimacy. First, when plebiscites are used to resolve territorial claims, particularly those involving different ethnic groups, the state controlling the plebiscite area enjoys an important advantage in gaining a favorable result in the election.[9] Therefore, there will probably be few territorial changes involving plebiscites, as the status quo is likely to be confirmed in any vote. This expectation is confirmed by noting that only three of the territorial changes here involved a plebiscite. Even were there not the problems stated above, there would still not be enough statistical variation to perform a meaningful analysis.

Although approval by the inhabitants of a territory may be a dimension of legitimacy, territorial transactions occur between states, not by the will of the people in the territory affected. Part of the legitimacy of the territorial change might be the degree of acceptance by the losing side. Frequently, agreement is signified by a formal instrument (that is, a treaty) transferring jurisdiction over the territory; the purchase of land is a common example. In theory, formal agreements represent a state's willingness to enter into the conditions of the contract and abide by its provisions. Thus, one might expect that territorial change formalized by a treaty would be regarded as legitimate by the gaining and losing sides (the gaining side must be considered in part because many territorial disputes are settled through compromise in which neither side's claims are fully satisfied). The norms of international law reinforce this perception.

Nevertheless, what may seem to be an obvious conclusion turns out to be a misleading one. A large number of treaties transferring territories are those entered into by something other than free will by the losing side. Some treaties are imposed on defeated states at the conclusion of wars and do not represent approval by the losing side, although they are technically binding on all parties under international law; Germany and the Versailles Treaty is the example that has received the most international attention. At other times, the coercion involved may be less obvious, but just as effective, as when the threat of force or the actual use of force will occur if the land is not transferred by treaty. In addition, states may acquire land by prescription, in which continued occupation and acquiescence, but not a formal treaty, indicate acceptance by both parties.[10]

Thus, we hypothesize that the *absence* of a treaty is associated with the legitimacy of a territorial change. The resort to legalism seems to be a last resort when there are problems with the legitimacy of the transaction. The illegitimacy of the Versailles Treaty after World War I stands in stark contrast to the legitimacy and stability of the post-World War II order despite the absence of a comprehensive treaty.

We also measure the legitimacy of a territorial change by reference to whether military conflict was used in the exchange. If states were willing to fight for territorial or other claims in the past, they may still regard those claims as valid. The state that yielded the territory may feel wronged and regard the prior military conflict as an illegitimate means to extort territorial concessions; it may conclude that military action is the only means to redress grievances or extract compensation in some other form. Thus, we look at the existence of military conflict in the original territorial exchange to measure the legitimacy of that exchange with the expectation that prior violence will lead to future conflict between the same parties.

RELATIVE CAPABILITIES

The relative capabilities of the two sides are indicated by the direct resources each could bring to bear in a potential dispute. Thus, for our purposes here, we look to the military component of national capabilities, and use the indicators of the ratio of the military expenditures and military personnel for gaining side to the losing side. In order to pinpoint a relevant time, we look at the relative capabilities of the two sides at the time of the first future dispute, or in the case of no future disputes, 30 years following the territorial change (or by 1980 for post-1950 territorial changes).

CONFLICT

To measure future conflict, we look to the number of militarized disputes between the two parties in the 30 years following the territorial change. As above, we concentrate only on disputes in which one of the two states was a primary party to the dispute.[11] A summary of the indicators is given in Table 5.4.

As a means of combining the multiple indicators of some of our concepts and estimating their relationships to military conflict, we again use a LISREL model.[12] In the next section, we report the results of the measurement models and the success of our theoretical models in predicting the frequency of future conflict between parties to a territorial change.

Empirical Results

The results of the analysis are presented in Figure 5.2. As has been our convention, we will consider the results of the measurement models and those of the structural equation separately.

Table 5.4 Summary of Variables and Indicators

Latent Variable	Indicator	Operational Measure
Intrinsic Importance	Area	Size of the territory exchanged in square kilometers
	Population	Number of people living in the territory at the time of the exchange
Relational Importance	Land type	Homeland or colonial territory
	Proximity	Absence or presence of a common land boundary or separation across water of less than 150 statute miles with the territory exchanged
Legitimacy	Previous Military Conflict	Absence or presence of military conflict in the territorial change
	Treaty	Absence or presence of a treaty in the territorial change
Relative Capabilities	Military Expenditures	Ratio of military expenditures of the gaining side to the losing side
	Military Personnel	Ratio of military personnel of the gaining side to the losing side

MEASUREMENT MODELS

The far right portion of Figure 5.2 reveals that the measurement models are, on the whole, quite successful. The coefficients for intrinsic importance demonstrate that population is a better indicator than area, but the latter is still related to the latent variable (as indicated by the R^2 value of .46). The measurement of relational importance is even more impressive. Both the type of territory exchanged and its geographic proximity to the gaining side are strongly related to the latent relational importance variable for the gaining side. The relational importance variable for the losing side required some modification. The two indicators were very highly correlated ($r=.98$) and therefore the measurement model could not be estimated. Thus, we relied only on the land type variable when measuring the relational importance of the losing side.

The relative power variable is well estimated by reference to military expenditures and military personnel. The two legitimacy indicators (treaty and previous military conflict) had to be considered separately as they constituted different dimensions of the concept. As there is only one indicator for each dimension of legitimacy, there is no empirical measurement error. Because of well-defined models and/or the use of single indicators for some of the latent variables, the measurement models are well specified. In the next section we discuss how well these variables predict future military conflict.

STRUCTURAL EQUATION

We now direct our attention to the right side of Figure 5.2. The model performs well in explaining the frequency of military conflict; the R^2 value is .48. Looking at the individual variables, we were unable to conduct significance tests using maximum likelihood (ML) estimates because of problems with "missing data," but we can compare the direction and relative strength of each variable, the latter by reference to the standardized coefficients.

The intrinsic importance of the territory is moderately related to the frequency of future conflict. The more value the territory has, the greater the frequency of militarized disputes between the parties to the territorial exchange. Yet, a comparison of the standardized coefficients reveals that the greatest effect is from the relational importance. As hypothesized, the loss of territory that has strong importance is a good predictor of future conflict; in our model, this has the greatest impact on the incidence of militarized disputes, as indicated by the standardized coefficient of 1.4. Thus, the importance of the territory, as we have stressed throughout the book, is again a significant predictor of military conflict, this time capable of explaining conflict over the 30 years after the event in question.

The relative importance of the territory to the gaining side is also a significant factor in future conflict, but in a manner opposite

Figure 5.2 LISREL Model of Territorial Changes and Recurring Conflict

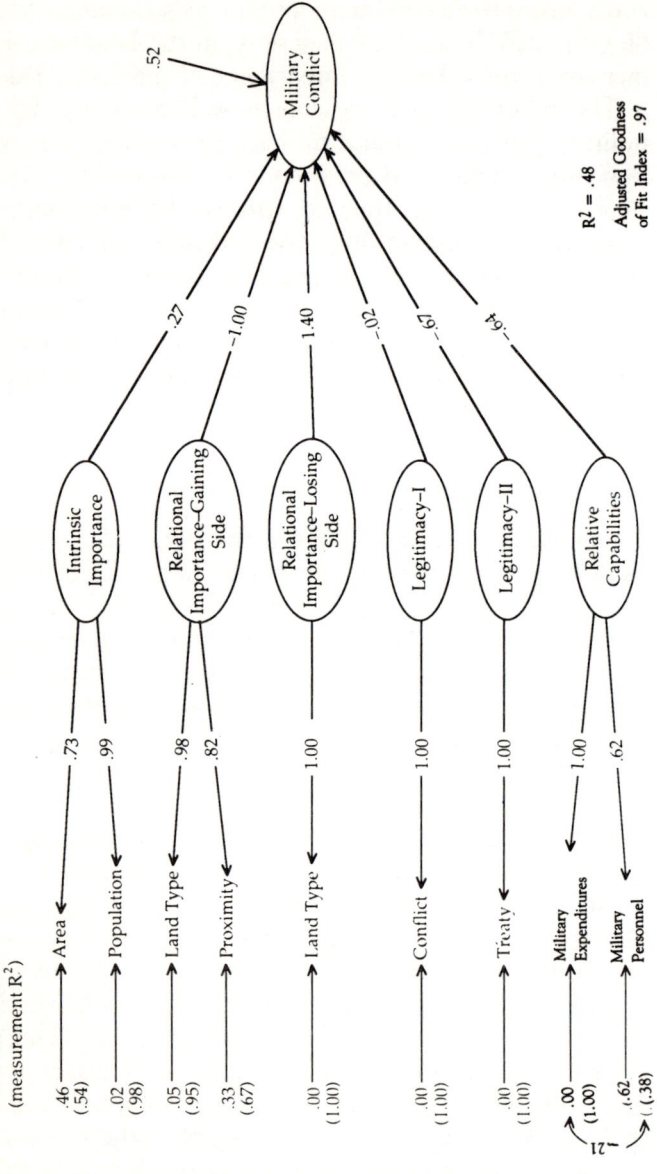

of what might be expected. The sign of the coefficient is negative (−1.0), suggesting that future conflict is more likely when the territory is *less* important to the gaining side. There are several explanations for this puzzling finding. First, the relationship of the territory to the losing side was probably more important than to the gaining side. Thus, one might suspect that this finding may be indicative of only a spurious relationship. More likely, the losing state will not risk a dispute with the gaining side if that gaining side considers the territory important and is stronger than the losing side. The losing side may only fight over important territory, but not if its opponent is also likely to resist such action and the opponent is militarily superior. Thus, the losing side is deterred from engaging in hostilities.

The importance of relative capabilities is confirmed when looking at Figure 5.2. The results are consistent with the original expectations and with the above explanation of our relational importance results. The negative coefficient (−.64) indicates that future conflict is more likely when the losing side has a military advantage. This confirms our belief that the losing side must have the opportunity, as well as the willingness, to redress grievances. It also suggests that it will not pursue claims against a stronger rival who also has strong incentives to resist.

The legitimacy of the territorial change also influences the likelihood of future military conflict. In particular, the presence of a treaty was positively related to future conflict. Nevertheless, we must exercise caution in interpreting these results. Our other measure of legitimacy, previous military conflict, was unrelated to future conflict. Furthermore, we acknowledged earlier the difficulty of finding indicators for the concept of legitimacy and our measures here may be inadequate or misleading.

Overall, the results are strong for the issues that concern us most in this book: the importance attached to a territory by a state is a significant predictor of military conflict.[13]

Conclusion

We were concerned with the extent to which territorial changes conditioned the likelihood and extent of future military conflict between the parties to that exchange. Almost 40 percent of the parties to a territorial change meet in a militarized dispute within 30 years of that exchange. Some parties, as in the cases of Israel and her neighbors, and India and Pakistan, have clashed continually following exchanges of territory. Although, in part, this may be because the parties have regular contact with each other and hence more opportunity for interactions of all kinds, it does not account for why some exchanges are followed by peaceful interactions and others experience violent ones.

We hypothesized that the conditions surrounding the territorial change would affect the likelihood that the parties would clash in the future. Thus, we focused on how important the territory was, to the losing side in particular, and how legitimate that territorial transfer was perceived to be. The results were that the importance, both relational and intrinsic, of the territory influenced the likelihood of future conflict. Also significant were the relative capabilities of the two sides. When those capabilities were in favor of the losing side, then future conflict also became more likely. One might also note the strength of the findings even given the measurement problems associated with territorial importance and legitimacy. We have acknowledged throughout the book the limitations of our measures of importance and pointed out in this chapter the difficulty of measuring legitimacy. The results are consistent with an earlier body of work that says the incidence of future conflict is only weakly (at best) a function of previous conflict between two states.[14] Thus, our findings may be viewed more as a reaffirmation of those findings than as a true test of the effect of territorial change legitimacy on future conflict.

In one sense, it is almost counterintuitive that the results could be as strong as they are given that we focus almost exclusively on the conditions surrounding the territorial change, and all but ignore the structural, situational factors at the time of the future conflict. Indeed, one knows from the start that some future conflict is unrelated, implicitly or explicitly, to the previous territorial change. Furthermore, except for considering relative capabilities, no reference is made to other, traditional realpolitik concerns such as alliances or arms races. Yet, the results in which the model can account for almost half of the variance in future conflict implies that those territorial changes can be important in some cases. Furthermore, the data are *censored* as the post-1950 disputes have not had the full 30 years to experience a dispute, and hence the relationships may be underestimated. In a broader context, this suggests that these events are related over time, that *history* is important. This may seem like an obvious conclusion, but one too often forgotten in most empirical studies of international relations.

One of the strengths of the literature on the diffusion of war is its emphasis on the interrelatedness of conflict over time. One of its weaknesses is its inability to specify how this connection is made. Our findings indicate that one mechanism is continuing claims made to a piece of territory. Also, much of the diffusion literature fails to consider the future conditions that facilitate or hinder conflict. Our evidence on relative capabilities indicates that they are significant factors in the study of diffusion of conflict over time.

In the final chapter, we review some of our findings and discuss their relevance for determining the frequency and scope of territorial changes in the future as well as the military conflict that may accompany them.

Notes

1. An example of research that treats disputes or conflict events as independent occurrences is Bruce Bueno de Mesquita, *The War Trap* (New Haven: Yale University Press, 1981). In general, the only research that looks at the interdependence of conflict events is the *contagion* or *diffusion* literature whose purpose is to ascertain and explain the degree of the relationship between the events.
2. Russell Leng, "When Will They Ever Learn: Coercive Bargaining in Recurrent Crises," *Journal of Conflict Resolution* 27 (1983):379–419.
3. Pierre Allan, *Crisis Bargaining and the Arms Race: A Theoretical Model* (Cambridge, Mass.: Ballinger Publishing, 1983).
4. See Wayne Wickelgren, "Exponential Decay and Independence from Irrelevant Associations in Short-Term Recognition Memory for Serial Order," *Journal of Experimental Psychology* 73 (1967):165–171 and "Multitrace Strength Theory" in *Models of Human Memory*, ed. Donald Norman (New York: Academic Press, 1970), 65–102.
5. The cases we study are all territorial changes between two states, including those in which a state gains its independence and joins the international system. From that list of 437, we eliminated 22. All independences in which the state does not join the international system immediately, such as Argentina, which gained its independence in 1816, are excluded. Also, cases in which states disappear from the international system after the territorial change, such as those involving the Baltic states just before and during World War II, are excluded.
6. Charles Gochman and Zeev Maoz, "Militarized Interstate Disputes,

1816–1976: Procedures, Patterns, and Insights," *Journal of Conflict Resolution* 28 (1984):587.
7. This problem is known as one of *censored* data. It is quite common in medical research and there are special statistical techniques to deal with it, but unfortunately these are unavailable in the LISREL framework.
8. For a discussion of the coding, see Charles Gochman, "Interstate Metrics: Conceptualizing, Operationalizing, and Measuring the Geographic Proximity of States Since the Congress of Vienna," *International Interactions* (forthcoming).
9. J.R.V. Prescott, *The Geography of Frontiers and Boundaries* (Chicago: Aldine Publishing, 1965).
10. See Michael Akehurst, *A Modern Introduction to International Law*, 4th ed. (London: Allen and Unwin, 1982).
11. There are some cases in which the basic identity of the state is changed, making the coding of future conflict problematic. In the case of Austria-Hungary after World War I, we coded Austria as the successor state. More problematic is the breakup of Germany after World War II; we decided to code West Germany as the successor state.
12. The model was estimated using unweighted least squares from the correlation matrix estimated by LISREL. Because we have a number of ordinal categorical variables, there are certain problems in that LISREL assumes underlying continuous variables. It is reasonable to assume, however, that an interval scale underlies the variables estimated.
13. We attempted to predict the severity of the first dispute following the territorial change using the same model described in Figure 5.2, but these results were not significant. It seems that the prior territorial change was better able to predict the extent of a future militarized dispute than it was the behavior of the states in the first dispute.
14. For example, see Richard Stoll, "From Fire to Frying Pan: The Impact of Major Power War Involvement on Major Power Dispute Involvement," *Conflict Management and Peace Science* 7 (1984):71–82.

CHAPTER 6

Territorial Changes and the Future

At the outset of this book, we sought to demonstrate the importance of territorial control in international relations. The strategic, economic, political, and psychological benefits of territorial control are potentially great, as states have often clashed in attempts to retain, reassert, or acquire anew those benefits. One of the main goals of this book has been to understand when states will fight over the transfer of territory and when they can amicably resolve questions of territorial sovereignty. In doing so, we looked at 770 instances of territorial change in the international system over the 1816 to 1980 period.

Territorial changes since 1816 represent a diverse collection of phenomena. Included are sales of territory between friendly and unfriendly states, transfers of colonial and noncolonial territory, and transactions involving entities such as Zanzibar and other political groupings not recognized as states in the international system. About the only thing that all of these changes share is the participation of at least one recognized state as either the gaining or losing side. Slightly less than a third of these transfers involved military conflict between the gaining and losing sides in the transfer.

While recognizing the diversity of events in this collection, we focused our analysis on three subsets of phenomena. These might generally be considered the most important from the vantage point of understanding military conflict as well as for the development of the international system. First, we looked at territorial changes that involved a dependent territory gaining independence from an imperial/colonial power and joining the international system of states. After looking at the growth of the international system, we turned our attention to the most significant changes in the geographic configuration of the international system: transfers of homeland territory between states. In each of those sets of cases (chapters 3 and 4 respectively), we sought to understand when military conflict would be a part of those changes. In chapter 5, we focused on how territorial changes influenced the likelihood of future military conflict between the same pair of parties to the change.

The results of our efforts, if not always dramatic, were coherent and promising. We were able to explain 50 percent of the variance in the incidence of military conflict in cases of national independence. Our model focused on the importance of the territory exchanged, the power decline of the imperial/colonial state, and, most significantly, the prevailing norms in the international system. Beyond merely being different phenomena, the territorial changes of homeland areas are conditioned by different factors. Thus, although our model of military conflict in these kinds of territorial changes also includes territorial importance, other considerations were more relevant; these include expansionist pressures on the parties to the exchange and the relative power distribution between them. In this analysis, the results were less dramatic and the patterns of behavior varied over time.

Our final analysis looked at future conflict between the parties to a territorial exchange. By looking only at the characteristics of the exchange (in terms of territorial importance and the legitimacy of the exchange) and the relative capabilities of the two sides, we were able to model the frequency of military conflict between the two sides in the 30 years following the exchange.

We wish to discuss in more detail the findings of the three sets of analyses in the context of two theoretical concerns. These are the utility of a realpolitik view and the necessity of taking into account the importance of territorial issues. Understanding the value attached to territory is important in explaining the conditions associated with territorial changes and also in the broader context of international relations. Following these discussions, we turn our attention to the likelihood and configuration of future territorial changes, drawing on the insights gained from the analyses.

The Utility of Realpolitik

Most analyses of international conflict rely only on a range of variables (alliances, arms races) that represent different variations of the influence of power in accounting for state actions. That is, those studies make an a priori assumption that power concerns are the primary, if not the sole, motivation for state behavior. One can trace this back to the Realist paradigm,[1] in which nations are motivated by the pursuit of power, and the decision to fight or concede is one made on the basis of rational calculations of success (which are in turn based on the relative power of the state to its opponent).[2]

No one study can be said to judge fully the utility of the realpolitik approach and there are well developed critiques of the paradigm elsewhere.[3] Yet, the results do indicate how useful realpolitik concerns are in territorial conflict, and perhaps in international conflict of all varieties. In contrast to the traditional approaches, our models of territorial conflict include in each case at least one variable representing the influence of power considerations on state behavior. Also included in the models are variables representing factors not considered relevant to national decisions by the realpolitik approach; these include international norms, legitimacy, and the intrinsic and relational importance of the territory exchanged. This permits some comparisons of the importance of power politics variables relative to other factors in affecting decisions about conflict. Thus, the focus is directed, in a statistical sense, to whether the variables under scrutiny were significant (that is, can we say they actually influence behavior?) and, given significance, which exercise the greatest relative influence on behavior.

In each set of analyses (national independence, homeland exchanges, and recurring conflict), relative capabilities are a significant factor in understanding military conflict. With respect to national independence, the decline of an imperial/colonial power relative to its peers is a good predictor of whether one of its dependent territories receives independence peacefully. Correspondingly, nineteenth century territorial conflict between states is related to the relative power decline of the losing side (as indicated by the lack of expansionist pressures on that state) and most often involves military conflict when the gaining side has a power advantage. Looking into the future, military conflict between parties to a previous territorial exchange is more likely when the losing side gains the upper hand in military capabilities.

Only in twentieth century territorial changes between states do relative capabilities fail to exercise a significant impact on the likelihood of military conflict. In that set of cases, however, other variables indicating expansionist pressures on the gaining side in the exchange are significant; such predictions are largely consistent with the realpolitik approach in that economic and military growth (that is, increases in national capabilities) lead to the acquisition of more territory, which in turn further enhances the power of the state in question. A consistent finding throughout our analyses is that power politics factors do make a difference and exercise an impact on behavior largely consistent with that specified in prior research and in the realpolitik paradigm.

The above discussion suggests that the power politics approach has been validated and that territorial conflict can be properly viewed through its conceptual lenses. Yet, a closer look at the findings reveals the limitations of that approach along with its value. In the analysis of national independence cases, power decline is a significant factor in the likelihood of military conflict, but two other factors not included in the realpolitik view are also significant, and one (international norms) has a greater impact than power decline. The use of the concept of territorial importance and its broader implications for the consideration of issues and their salience are discussed more fully in the next section. States are influenced greatly by the international consensus on the need for decolonization. This leads them to give up dependent territories peacefully even though economic benefits are sacrificed in the process.

The realpolitik model assumes an inherent anarchy in the organization and structure of international relations. The idea that internationally shared standards of behavior (beyond those assumed by the approach) exist is not considered. Furthermore, that these standards should exercise a greater influence than the desire for enhancing and/or maintaining power is nothing short of heresy for realists. Our results suggest for this subset of cases that realpolitik concerns are significant, but secondary to other influences.

The other sets of cases similarly reveal the significance of power concerns, but also the relevance, and sometimes the primacy, of other factors. Conflict over exchanges of homeland territory are strongly influenced by realpolitik concerns, primarily the relative capabilities of the two sides and the expansionist pressures on those states. Yet, at least for the twentieth century cases, territorial importance also conditions the likelihood of military conflict. In cases of recurring conflict, the future distribution of power between the gaining and losing side is important in affecting future conflict, but the relational importance of the territory exchanged is more critical.

What all this suggests is that power politics concerns are critical components of models of territorial conflict, but they should not be the exclusive components. In our sets of cases, realpolitik concerns are less important when there are well-developed international standards of behavior and when the territory involved is not the homeland of the losing side. There are probably few examples in international relations of norms as well developed as the decolonization norm. Yet, in issue areas such as nuclear nonproliferation, international standards have emerged, are emerging, and in some cases are growing stronger. They must be accounted for in models of state behavior.

It is perhaps not surprising that realpolitik variables perform best in cases involving the exchange of homeland territory between states. There are few developed standards on how to handle such territorial disputes. This kind of territory has the greatest relational importance for states and they have resisted any attempts at the international level to influence or regulate activities within their home territory. Article 2 (7) of the United Nations Charter specifically limits the power of the organization to matters outside the domestic purview of the state. Yet, even in this domain in which the characterization of international anarchy best applies, the significance of territorial importance as a motivation for behavior again suggests the limitations of the realpolitik approach.

The results of the analyses are strong in cases of national independence and recurring conflict and more modest in our study of interstate transfers. In any event, we have a significant distance to go before accounting for all of the military conflict in territorial changes. One might argue that our models inadequately specified or measured the realpolitik variables that conditioned state decisions. Yet, this is a double-edged sword in that the same might be said of other nonrealpolitik variables. The significance of territorial importance and international norms cannot be dismissed by reference to the methodological problems with the power politics variables.

In the next section, we discuss our results on territorial importance for the study of territorial changes and, by implication, look at the relevance of issues and their salience in a dispute in order to understand and the use of military force. The conclusion is that further modifications must be made to the power politics approach.

Territorial Importance

One of the unifying themes of this book is the supposition that states choose to fight over territory in part because of the importance of that territory. We distinguish two kinds of territorial importance: intrinsic and relational. The former concerns the inherent value, usually economic, that a territory holds for any sovereign. Relational importance refers to the value that a territory has for a particular state (including strategic and ethnic concerns among others), with the recognition that this would vary, sometimes greatly, across states.

The results of the empirical analyses bear out our expectations. Territorial importance is significant in explaining military conflict in each of our sets of cases. The relative significance of the importance variables varies according to the problem studied. Territorial importance is strongest in predicting future conflict and weakest for military conflict over homeland territory. In part, this is due to the accuracy of measurement of the importance variables. The operational indicators of territorial importance vary according to the set of cases studied for conceptual reasons, but also because of methodological limitations. Territorial importance is only measured by the size of the area exchanged in the analyses of homeland territory exchanges. It may be surprising that, given such a limited variable, any significant results are obtained. Yet homeland territory has relational importance for both sides in these exchanges. There is not enough statistical variation to include relational importance in the model; yet, this set of cases as a whole has a higher frequency of military conflict than other types, suggesting that relational importance has an effect on decisions to use military force. When the measures for importance are better, as in the cases of national independence and recurring conflict, the results are more robust.

Another notable finding is that relational importance exercises a greater impact on the likelihood of military conflict than does intrinsic importance; this result is consistent in analyses that include both aspects of importance in models of conflict. We believe that such findings are not merely the product of measurement deficiencies.

Territorial Changes and the Future

While the intrinsic value of territory cannot be ignored, it seems to us that states are more concerned with the idiosyncratic benefits that are derived from owning a particular piece of land. Furthermore, states may be better able to recognize the relational importance of territory for security and economic benefits. The inherent value of a territory may not always be clear to a state and ultimately it may regard the individual benefits as more valuable than the often nonfungible attributes of the intrinsic importance of the land.

This has several implications. First, it suggests that the salience of a dispute will not be the same for all parties and can change over time. Operational measures of issue salience in scholarly research and dispute resolution proposals alike must account for these differences. Second, the different views on the salience of a dispute open up the possibility for misperception. States may underestimate the resolve of an opponent to acquire or defend a piece of territory because they do not see the land as vital or valuable. Third, it suggests that the resolution of territorial disputes may need more than a division of land area into equal pieces. Any territorial agreement must take into account the particular value that the area holds for each party in the dispute. It may be that security interests can be satisfied without a territorial change. Yet it also may be that the interests of the protagonists are incompatible such that any division of the disputed land will be unacceptable to one side or the other. The division of Palestine after World War II was based only on the intrinsic importance of the territory. Because the relational importance of the area was not considered, the partition did not bring the hoped for peace.

Table 6.1 Remaining Dependent Territories

Territory	Imperial/ Colonial Power	Population
American Samoa	United States	40,000
Anguila	United Kingdom	6,500
Aruba	Netherlands	67,000
Ashmore and Cartier Is.	Australia	—
Bakers, Howard, and Jarvis Is.	United States	—
Bermuda	United Kingdom	63,000
British Indian Ocean Territory	United Kingdom	2,000

Table 6.1 continued

British Virgin Is.	United Kingdom	12,034
Canton and Enderbury Is.	United States and United Kingdom	—
Cayman Is.	United Kingdom	18,000
Channel Is.	United Kingdom	130,000
Christmas Is.	Australia	3,094
Cook Is.	New Zealand	20,000
Coral Sea Is.	Australia	—
Falkland Is.	United Kingdom	2,000
French Polynesia	France	160,000
Gibraltar	United Kingdom	30,000
Greenland	Denmark	51,000
Guam	United States	120,000
Heard and McDonald Is.	Australia	—
Hong Kong	United Kingdom	5,420,000
Isle of Man	United Kingdom	60,000
Johnston Atoll	United States	300
Kingman Reef	United States	—
Macau	Portugal	390,000
Mayotte	France	53,000
Midway Is.	United States	2,200
Montserrat	United Kingdom	12,160
Namibia	South Africa	1,510,000
Netherlands Antilles	Netherlands	200,000
New Caledonia	France	150,000
Niue	New Zealand	6,000
Norfolk Is.	Australia	2,175
Pitcairn Is.	United Kingdom	68
Puerto Rico	United States	3,270,000
St Helena, Ascension, Tristan da Cunha	United Kingdom	6,000
Swan Is.	United States	—
Tokelau	New Zealand	1,552
Trust Territory of the Pacific Is.	United States	116,974
Turks and Caicos Is.	United Kingdom	7,000
U.S. Virgin Is.	United States	95,951
Wake Is.	United States	1,600
Wallis and Futuna Is.	France	11,943

Source: Martin Glassner and Harm de Blij, *Systematic Political Geography*, 4th ed. New York: John Wiley, 1989, p. 308. Reprinted with permission.

In summary, scholars and decision-makers alike must take into account the perceived importance of a territory in assessing the probability of national decisions to use military force. Consideration must be given to both the importance of a territory in the eye of the beholder and the idea that different states will view different areas with varying degrees of importance.

New States and the Expansion of the International System

As was discussed in chapters 2 and 3, the size of the international system grew dramatically after World War II, with the number of states almost tripling. Nevertheless, there are no longer uncharted areas of the globe to be explored. Other than the polar regions (which are the subject of some international agreements[4]), most land masses have at least some effective occupation. This may suggest that the rapid expansion of the international system is over and that the number of states in the international system has approached some limit. There are, however, two primary routes of expansion for the international system: the formation of states from current dependent territories and the formation of new states by secession from existing states. In this section, we consider these possibilities and discuss the likelihood that the process will involve military conflict.

Most of the growth in the international system over the past 175 years has come by way of the decolonization process, as dependent territories gained their independence. In the coming years, this is unlikely to be repeated. Glassner and De Blij identified 43 remaining dependent territories at the beginning of 1989.[5] These are listed in Table 6.1. From that list, we can begin to assess whether independences are likely and whether they will involve military conflict. One might immediately note that the disposition of two of the territories is apparently settled: Namibia and Hong Kong.

At this writing, Namibia has successfully completed elections to form a new, majority-rule government and it has joined the international system as an independent state. Independence from South Africa came after years of international pressure and considerable violence, the latter characterized by numerous clashes

135

between the South African army and troops from the South West African Peoples Organization (SWAPO). One part of our analysis would seem to imply that any new independences would be free from military conflict given the strong international norm of decolonization. Yet a closer look reveals that military conflict in Namibia is not so surprising. Despite a strong international norm of decolonization, South Africa has consistently and vociferously resisted international pressure for years. In effect, while the international norm was strong, it had not been internalized by the state it was supposed to influence. Indeed, one might argue that South Africa has been the state most resistant to international pressure and standards since 1945. This is not to say that economic sanctions, sports boycotts, and other international pressures had no effect, but rather that alone they could not force the South African government to grant independence.

Our model of military conflict in cases of national independence also indicates the relevance of territorial importance in decisions of the colonial/imperial power to resist independence efforts. In the case of Namibia, its importance to South Africa made that state more willing to fight for its retention. Namibia includes large deposits of strategic minerals giving it great intrinsic importance. The size of the land area and its population made it one of the largest remaining dependent territories. In addition, it has great relational importance to the South Africans. As a bordering area, it provides a buffer against hostile front-line states. The presence of Walvis Bay, a deep water port, in Namibia[6] is also very important economically. Thus, international norms were not effective restraints on South Africa and the value of Namibia made military conflict a reality before the South African regime finally gave up control of the territory.

With respect to Hong Kong, an agreement has been reached for Britain to relinquish control of the area, but it will not become an independent state. Rather, it will become incorporated into the homeland territory of the People's Republic of China. This reveals a significant point about dependent territories—they are not all destined to become independent states. Besides Hong Kong, several other dependent territories might just as easily be incorporated into existing states as become new sovereignties. There are competing political movements in Puerto Rico to make that island an independent nation-state, the 51st member of the United States, and to retain its current status. Which one will ultimately succeed is unclear. Furthermore, should the British relinquish control of the Falkland Islands or Gibraltar, it is unlikely that either would become a separate state; most likely Argentina and Spain, respectively, would incorporate them.

The remaining dependent territories are small islands with tiny populations. Many of these islands could not function as independent states. A few lack the basic prerequisite for statehood: a permanent population. Others could not effectively carry out foreign policy or other duties and might be relegated to a status similar to that of Monaco or San Marino. With the exception of New Calendonia perhaps, most small dependent territories do not have any indigenous movements for independence and may not have any desire for it any time in the near future.

Overall, we might expect few of the dependent territories on the list to become independent states before the turn of the century. Should any occur, however, we might expect those transitions to be peaceful. The international norm of decolonization is a strong one and likely to exercise a powerful restraint on the remaining imperial/colonial powers. Furthermore, most of the territories are not valuable from an intrinsic or relational point of view and thus would not prompt battles over their status even as the United States, Britain, France, and others decline in relative power.

Although the explosion of new states from decolonization is unlikely to be repeated, the international system might still expand through the secession of territories to form new states. Historically though, secession is relatively uncommon, constituting less than 5 percent of the cases of territorial change since 1815. Even rarer have been the cases of secession involving military conflict since 1945. Only Bangladesh in recent memory was successful in breaking away by the use of military force, and then only with the assistance of India. If the future follows the past, one might expect few cases of secession in the coming years.

There are several reasons, however, to expect that secessionist movements may become more common and perhaps more successful. There is certainly no shortage of national and ethnic groups clamoring for states of their own. On almost every continent, at least one group seeks to break away and form a new independent state. Indeed, the way the map of Africa was drawn all but invites such claims. The ongoing civil war in Ethiopia between the government and the Eritrean rebels is an example. Yet, perhaps surprisingly, secessionist movements flourish more on other continents, most notably Europe. The reform movement in Eastern Europe has unleashed pent-up nationalist feelings and various ethnic and national groups are demanding greater autonomy or independence from their home states. Yugoslavia runs the risk of breaking into independent states along ethnic lines and Czechoslovakia and Romania face similar difficulties.

Perhaps nowhere are nationalist tensions greater than in the Soviet Union. Soviet republics are a diverse mixture of territories gained through expansion, historical areas identified with Mother Russia, and former sovereign states absorbed during war. Southern republics, which have large Muslim populations, were the scene of violent clashes in the early 1990s, with some local groups calling for independence. More seriously, the former states of Lithuania, Latvia, and Estonia seek to regain their sovereignty. In March 1990, Lithuania unilaterally declared its independence. Whether these events signal a general breakup of the Soviet Union is not clear at this writing.

Part of the growth of secessionist movements in recent times can be attributed to the breakdown of authority structures within states. Rosenau has noted that while states have become more interdependent externally, they have become less effective internally.[7] There is a tendency toward fragmentation with many subgroups arising, often possessing considerable resources. When there is greater coherence of a subsystem, the system as a whole tends to experience problems. In this case, ethnic and religious ties (sometimes reinforcing each other) have made the breakup of states a more likely occurrence in the coming years than had been true in the past.

It is conceivable that a number of new states may be formed out of the territory of existing system members. Yet, one might expect that the process will be a relatively peaceful one. Given the strength of the host states, most violent efforts at secession are likely to meet the fate that the Biafrans experienced in their unsuccessful attempt to break away from Nigeria. Nevertheless, few predicted the growth of new states after World War II and it is always difficult to forecast future trends, much less make predictions on individual cases.

Although secession and the freeing of dependent territories are the most likely ways the size of the international system will change, there are a few other possibilities. It may be that a new Palestinian state will be formed out of the territory occupied by Israel after the 1967 war. As organized violence has occurred consistently since the beginning of that occupation, there is little reason to believe that a new Palestinian state (if one emerges at all) will do so after a prolonged period of peace.

The other possibility is that the international system will contract through the unification of several members of the system. Again this has been a rare occurrence, primarily taking place as modern Italy and Germany were formed in the nineteenth century. Later attempts at unification, such as the ill-fated United Arab Republic, were short-lived. Moves toward a more united European Community might represent a new trend toward regional integration. Nevertheless, even economic integration in 1992 will have its difficulties, and political integration at this writing seems far off. Other attempts at regional integration in Africa and Latin America that focused on economic or cultural affairs never got off the ground. Thus, regional integration efforts are unlikely to change dramatically the size or shape of the international system.

Any unification efforts are likely to take place in so-called divided states. Vietnam in 1975 is a recent example of a state restoring its unity following an ideological division of its boundaries. There are still other states that remain artifacts of the Cold War. The Taiwan–China and North Korea–South Korea divisions are candidates for reunification if significant political hurdles are cleared. The most obvious case of a divided state is Germany. It took only the opening of the Berlin Wall to expose reunification feelings suppressed for 45 years. Nevertheless, divided states are anomalies in the international system and they are slowly becoming anachronisms. Their future impact on the size of the international system will be minimal, although their political and military impact may be great.

In a sense, one chapter of the territorial history of the international system is over. It is unlikely that new areas or populations will be brought into the state system. Yet, the number of states may grow slightly or, in rare instances, contract. It is difficult to believe, however, that the days of booming growth in the number of states in the system during the 1950s and 1960s will be repeated in the next decades. Any changes that do occur though will likely be completed peacefully given the strong international norms, the absence of remaining important dependent territories, and the ability of states to put down secession attempts. What is left to be written is how the configuration of the state system will change as its members battle over disputed territories. We address that issue in the next section.

Changes in the Configuration of the International System

We stated in chapter 4 that territorial changes involving the homeland of the gaining and losing sides have a greater propensity for military conflict than other kinds of exchanges; this is perhaps the result of homeland territory being regarded as very important by both sides and hence worth fighting for. There remain a number of territorial disputes today that involve conflicting claims over homeland territory. Those identified by Day in a survey of border and territorial disputes are given in Table 6.2.[8]

An overview of this list reveals territorial disputes in every region and involving a variety of countries. Most of the European disputes seem to trace their origins to the post-World War II redistribution of land. For most of the postwar era, one assumed that the division of Germany and the distribution of German lands to Poland were realities that would not change easily or quickly. Yet, few foresaw the destruction of the Berlin Wall in 1989. Most were equally surprised by the banners greeting West German Chancellor Helmut Kohl as he visited Silesia, a former German territory now part of Poland, that same year: "Helmut, You're Our Chancellor Too."[9] Other territorial disputes seem the result of the division of ethnic minorities across national boundaries. Complaints about forced assimilation and calls for autonomy have characterized the disputes between Hungary and Romania, and Albania and Yugoslavia.

Ethnic conflicts also characterize the territorial disputes of Africa. As noted above, colonial boundaries, sometimes drawn without regard to tribal boundaries, formed the basis for state boundaries when those territories gained their independence. This has caused problems when a tribal group exists as a minority in one state rather than being united with other tribal members who are in the majority in another state; Somalian claims to part of Ethiopia fit this pattern. Several other disputes are remnants of colonialism, as new states claim island territories still held by their former imperial/colonial

Territorial Changes and the Future

power (for example, France and Mauritius's dispute over Tromelin Island).

It may be surprising that territorial conflict in the Middle East includes more than the Arab–Israeli rivalry. Most disputes in the region involve competing claims over minor border areas or islands.

Table 6.2 Current Territorial Disputes

Region	States	Territory
Europe		
	Albania–Greece	Northern Epirus
	Albania–Yugoslavia	Kosovo
	Austria–Italy	South Tyrol
	Finland–Sweden	Aaland Is.
	Germany–Poland	Poland/Germany
	Hungary–Romania	Northern Transylvania
	United Kingdom–Ireland	Northern Ireland
	Italy–Yugoslavia	Trieste
	Greece–Bulgaria –Yugoslavia	Macedonia
	Romania–Soviet Union	Moldavia
	Spain–United Kingdom	Gibraltar
Africa		
	Cameroon–Nigeria	border area
	Chad–Libya	Aozuo Strip
	Chad–Nigeria	Lake Chad Is.
	Comoros–France	Mayotte Is.
	Ethiopia–Somalia	Ogaden
	France–Madagascar	Is. of Madagascar
	France–Mauritius	Tromelin Is.
	Ghana–Togo	Togo
	Kenya–Somalia	N.E. Kenya
	Lesotho–South Africa	border area
	Malawi–Tanzania	Lake Nyasa
	Malawi–Zambia	border area
	Mauritius–United Kingdom	Diego Garcia
	Morocco–Spain	Spanish enclaves and Is.
	South Africa–Swaziland	Ingwavuma and KwaZulu
	Zaire–Zambia	Lake Mueru
Middle East		
	Arab States–Israel	Palestine/Israel
	Bahrein–Iran	Bahrein
	Bahrein–Qatar	Hawar Is.
	Egypt–Israel	Taba Strip
	Iran–Iraq	Shat al-Arab
	Iran–United Arab Emirates	Strait of Hormuz Is.

141

Table 6.2 continued

	Iraq–Kuwait	Kuwait
	Kuwait–Saudi Arabia	Persian Gulf Is.
	Syria–Turkey	Hatay
Asia		
	Afghanistan–Pakistan	border area
	Bangladesh–India	New Moore Is.
	Bhutan–China	border area
	China–India	border area
	China–Japan–Taiwan	Senkaku Is.
	China–Soviet Union	border area
	China–Taiwan	Taiwan
	China–Vietnam	border area and Is.
	France–Vanuatu	Matthew and Hunter Is.
	India–Pakistan	Kashmir
	Indonesia–Portugal	East Timor
	Japan–South Korea	Tokto
	Japan–Soviet Union	several islands
	North Korea–South Korea	Korea
	Laos–Thailand	border area
	Malaysia–Philippines	Sabah
	China–Tawain–Vietnam –Philippines–Malaysia	Spratly Is.
Americas		
	Argentina–Paraguay	border area
	Argentina–United Kingdom	Falkland Is.
	Belize–Guatemala	Belize
	Bolivia–Chile	Lauca River
	Bolivia–Chile–Peru	War of the Pacific claims
	Colombia–Nicaragua	Caribbean archipelago
	Colombia–Venezuela	Los Monjes Is.
	Ecuador–Peru	Amazon Basin
	El Salvador–Honduras	border area
	France–Suriname	Maroni river area
	Guyana–Suriname	Corentyne river area
	Guyana–Venezuela	Essequibo river area
	Haiti–United States	Navassa Is.
	Argentina–United Kingdom –Chile–France–Australia –New Zealand–Norway	Antarctica

Source: Derived from Alan Day (ed.), *Border and Territorial Disputes*, 2nd ed. Essex: Longman, 1987.

In Asia, China has disputes with most of her neighbors. Most of the other major actors in the area (Pakistan, India, Vietnam, and Japan) also have their share of competing territorial claims. Territorial disputes in the Western Hemisphere are again boundary line disputes usually involving small areas.

Although territorial disputes are numerous, it does not mean that alteration of state borders through violence is likely in many, most, or all cases. Many of the disputes are long-standing, suggesting that states have been reluctant, because of deterrence or other more benign reasons, to use military force to press their claims. In several instances in which states did try to alter boundary lines through military force, the attempts failed. Libya's occupation of Northern Chad and Somalia's seizure of the Ogaden were ultimately defeated and resulted in no permanent territorial gains. Other territorial disputes also linger after unsuccessful attempts to seize disputed areas, such as the Iran–Iraq dispute.

Our analyses do not permit us to identify when states will try to fight for territorial claims. Rather, we can only provide insights into whether future territorial change might involve military conflict. From that perspective, it appears unlikely that many territorial changes in the coming decades will be violent ones. Most of the disputed areas are small in size and without great economic value; this suggests that states may not be willing to bear the costs of military conflict in order to acquire the territories. Nevertheless, several claims based on ethnic or national grounds, such as the Arab–Israeli conflict and the dispute between Belize and Guatemala, have the greatest likelihood of military conflict. International standards to preserve current boundaries seem to be strongest in Africa with a formal agreement not to alter boundary lines by force. In other regions, there are less formal standards for observing the status quo, but there are organizations (such as the OAS) that act as a restraint on territorial ambitions.

As is evident from our description and analyses, not all territorial changes occur after protracted and competing claims over land areas. Historically, many territorial changes were the products of major power war; virtually all types of territorial changes, homeland changes in particular, followed such wars. We will not speculate on the likelihood of such an occurrence, but if the "long peace" persists and/or if major war is indeed obsolete,[10] then wholesale changes in the configuration of the international system are unlikely. The other source of territorial changes was expansionist pressures, especially population pressures. That might suggest that countries in Africa or large states such as India or China would be good candidates for acquiring more territory through military means. That the latter two states have many ongoing territorial disputes makes such a possibility more realistic, although still speculative.

Many of the ongoing territorial disputes reported in Table 6.2 are reflections of dissatisfaction with previous territorial changes. Predicting future military conflict between states is a tenuous exercise. At best, we can offer a few guidelines for decision-makers in order to avoid future conflict after a territorial change, although even these are somewhat limited. Decision-makers can do little about the importance of a territory when a transfer of sovereignty takes place. Yet, the gaining side might recognize that because of location or historical ties, the losing side may be resentful of the loss of territory. Too often, leaders project their own perceptions and values on their counterparts in foreign capitals. Preventing future conflict may necessitate not acquiring the territory to begin with, as the benefits of acquiring the territory may be outweighed by future costs of conflict in defense of the territory. Israel's acquisition of the West Bank has been, in retrospect, a costly decision. In any case, when important territory is transferred, diplomatic efforts may have to be redoubled to head off future conflict. To continue with the Middle East example, a return of the lands occupied by Israel after the 1967 War might have to be accompanied by appropriate international guarantees, forces, and mechanisms for resolving future disagreements over the territories.

As we noted in chapter 5, plebiscites are not necessarily a desirable way to facilitate territorial changes and prevent recurring conflict. Plebiscites have become a virtually extinct practice in international relations. Were they to occur, they would probably favor the status quo, and shifting populations and uneven population growth in the territory affected render any guarantee against future disputes ineffective. Similarly, treaties are no indication that peace will prevail in the future. Decision-makers should not be misled by the presence of a written document. Historically, there has been some measure of coercion involved in the signing of most treaties. In addition, treaties have proved inadequate substitutes for true legitimacy. The other indicator of future conflict is a rise in the relative capabilities of the losing side in the exchange. At this stage, the gaining side may need to take compensatory action such as enhancing its own capabilities through alliances or military buildups. In general, our analysis provides some early warning indicators, not practical solutions, for dealing with the problem of recurring conflict.

Over 50 years ago, Spykman noted that geography is the most fundamentally conditioning factor in the foreign policy of states because it is the most permanent.[11] In our analysis, it has been changes in that geography, which are largely defined by the actions of nation-states, that have been an integral part of international relations. In that sense, it has been its mutability, not its static qualities, that have given geography its importance.

Notes

1. Hans Morgenthau, *Politics Among Nations*, 3rd ed. (New York: Alfred Knopf, 1960).
2. Yet the capabilities of a state are not always related to its ability to influence foreign policy outcomes. This is most evident in the so-called *power paradox* in which big states lose little wars. For a discussion, see Zeev Maoz, "Power, Capabilities, and Paradoxical Conflict Outcomes," *World Politics* 41 (1989):239–266 and James Lee Ray and Ayse Vural, "Power Disparities and Paradoxical Conflict Outcomes," *International Interactions* 12 (1986):315–342.
3. For example, see John Vasquez, *The Power of Power Politics* (New Brunswick: Rutgers University Press, 1981).
4. The Antarctic Treaty of 1959 allows no new territorial claims there and allows equal access to all signatories while not resolving the validity of any previous territorial claims in the area.
5. Martin Glassner and Harm de Blij, *Systematic Political Geography*, 4th ed. (New York: John Wiley, 1989), 308.
6. There is considerable controversy over whether Walvis Bay should be considered a part of Namibia. South Africa has long contended that the bay is their own territory, and therefore not subject to the disposition of the Namibian territory, despite the absence of geographic contiguity to the South African homeland.
7. James Rosenau, "A Pre-Theory Revisited: World Politics in an Era of Cascading Interdependence," *International Studies Quarterly* 28 (1984):245–305; James Rosenau, "The State in an Era of Cascading Politics: Wavering Concept, Widening Competence, Withering Colossus, or Weathering Change?," *Comparative Political Studies* 21 (1988):13–44; James Rosenau, "Patterned Chaos in Global Life: Structure and Process in the Two Worlds of World Politics," *International Political Science Review* 9 (1988):327–364.

8. Alan Day, ed., *Border and Territorial Disputes*, 2nd ed. (Essex: Longman, 1987).
9. "Kohl, Visiting Land Lost to Poles, Hears Reconciliation Mass," *New York Times*, 13 November 1989, p. 1.
10. John Mueller, *Retreat from Doomsday: The Obsolescence of Major War* (New York: Basic Books, 1989).
11. Nicholas Spykman, "Geography and Foreign Policy, I," *American Political Science Review* 32 (1938):28–50.

APPENDIX

Territorial Changes, 1816 to 1980

Listed below are the 770 cases of territorial changes that form the basis for the analyses in the book. The states or political entities involved as the gaining and losing sides are presented. In most cases we used the name of the entity at the time of the exchange. Several states changed their names or had successor states with different names. Accordingly, we use the name Ottoman Empire until 1918 and Turkey thereafter, Russia until 1918 and Soviet Union thereafter, Serbia until 1945 and Yugoslavia thereafter, Prussia until 1867 and Germany thereafter, and Piedmont until 1860 and Italy thereafter. We also list the name or location of the unit of territory exchanged. There we list the name of the territory at the time of the exchange or its contemporary name if this was more familiar to the reader. We should note that the unit exchanged may refer to all or part of that unit.

Case #	Year	Gaining Side	Losing Side	Unit Exchanged
1	1816	Argentina	Spain	Argentina
2	1816	United Kingdom	none	Gambia
3	1816	United Kingdom	Nepal	Nepal
4	1817	France	United Kingdom	Senegal
5	1817	Russia	none	Russia
6	1818	United States	United Kingdom	Canada
7	1818	Chile	Spain	Chile
8	1818	United Kingdom	none	India
9	1818	United Kingdom	none	Guinea
10	1818	United Kingdom	United States	United States
11	1818	Ottoman Empire	none	Hejez Sultanate
12	1819	United States	Spain	Cuba
13	1819	Colombia	Spain	Colombia
14	1819	France	Malagasy	Malagasy
15	1821	Dominican Rep.	Spain	Dominican Rep.
16	1821	Mexico	Spain	Mexico

147

Case #	Year	Gaining Side	Losing Side	Unit Exchanged
17	1821	Colombia	Spain	Venezuela
18	1821	Peru	Spain	Peru
19	1821	Portugal	Spain	Uruguay
20	1822	Colombia	Spain	Ecuador
21	1822	Ottoman Empire	none	Sudan
22	1824	Brazil	Portugal	Brazil
23	1824	United Kingdom	none	Singapore
24	1824	United Kingdom	Netherlands	Straits Settle.
25	1824	Netherlands	United Kingdom	Indonesia
26	1825	Bolivia	Spain	Bolivia
27	1825	United Kingdom	none	Bouvet
28	1825	Malagasy	France	Malagasy
29	1825	Tunisia	Ottoman Empire	Tunisia
30	1826	United Kingdom	none	Cape Colony
31	1826	United Kingdom	none	Malay States
32	1826	United Kingdom	Burma	Burma
33	1828	Uruguay	Brazil	Uruguay
34	1828	Netherlands	none	West Irian
35	1828	Greece	Ottoman Empire	Greece
36	1828	Russia	Iran	Iran
37	1829	United Kingdom	Spain	Fernando Po
38	1829	Russia	none	Russia
39	1829	Russia	Ottoman Empire	Ottoman Empire
40	1830	Belgium	Netherlands	Belgium
41	1830	France	Ottoman Empire	Algeria
42	1830	Russia	none	Russia
43	1832	Colombia	Ecuador	Ecuador
44	1833	United Kingdom	Argentina	Falkland Is.
45	1835	United Kingdom	none	Cape Colony
46	1836	Texas	Mexico	Texas
47	1839	Peru	Bolivia	Peru
48	1839	United Kingdom	none	Yemen
49	1839	United Kingdom	Sikkim	Sikkim
50	1839	Netherlands	none	Indonesia
51	1839	Belgium	Netherlands	Belgium
52	1839	Belgium	Netherlands	Luxembourg
53	1840	United Kingdom	none	New Zealand
54	1840	Portugal	none	Angola
55	1841	France	none	Comoros
56	1842	United States	United Kindgom	Canada
57	1842	United Kingdom	United States	United States
58	1842	United Kingdom	China	Hong Kong
59	1842	France	none	Polynesia
60	1843	United Kingdom	Natal	Natal
61	1843	United Kingdom	Sind	Sind
62	1843	Netherlands	none	Indonesia
63	1843	France	none	Ivory Coast

Appendix

Case #	Year	Gaining Side	Losing Side	Unit Exchanged
64	1843	Spain	United Kingdom	Fernando Po
65	1844	France	none	Polynesia
66	1845	United States	Texas	Texas
67	1845	France	none	Gabon
68	1846	United States	United Kingdom	Canada
69	1846	United Kingdom	United States	United States
70	1846	Austria-Hungary	Crakow	Crakow
71	1847	United Kingdom	none	South Africa
72	1847	United Kingdom	Brunei	Labuan
73	1847	France	none	Algeria
74	1847	Tuscany	Lucca	Lucca
75	1848	United States	Mexico	Mexico
76	1849	United Kingdom	Punjab	Punjab
77	1849	United Kingdom	Kashmir	Kashmir
78	1849	France	none	Guinea
79	1849	Prussia	Hohenzollern	Hohenzollern
80	1850	United Kingdom	Denmark	Ghana
81	1851	Brazil	Uruguay	Uruguay
82	1851	United Kingdom	Aden Prot.	Aden Prot.
83	1851	Netherlands	Portugal	Indonesia
84	1852	United Kingdom	Burma	Burma
85	1852	Transvaal	United Kingdom	Transvaal
86	1853	United States	Mexico	Mexico
87	1853	France	none	New Caledonia
88	1853	Russia	none	Russia
89	1854	United Kingdom	Oman	Oman
90	1854	Russia	none	Russia
91	1854	Orange Free St.	United Kingdom	Orange Free St.
92	1855	Egypt	Ottoman Empire	Egypt
93	1856	Ottoman Empire	Russia	Russia
94	1856	Ottoman Empire	Russia	Russia
95	1857	United Kingdom	none	Cocos Is.
96	1858	United States	none	Johnson Is.
97	1858	France	none	Polynesia
98	1858	Russia	none	Russia
99	1858	Russia	China	China
100	1859	Honduras	United Kingdom	Honduras
101	1859	Brazil	Venezuela	Venezuela
102	1859	Netherlands	Portugal	Indonesia
103	1859	Portugal	Netherlands	Timor
104	1859	Piedmont	Austria-Hungary	Austria-Hungary
105	1859	Russia	none	Russia
106	1860	Nicaragua	United Kingdom	Nicaragua
107	1860	United Kingdom	China	Hong Kong
108	1860	France	none	West Africa
109	1860	France	Italy	Italy
110	1860	Spain	Morocco	Ifni

Territorial Changes and International Conflict

Case #	Year	Gaining Side	Losing Side	Unit Exchanged
111	1860	Italy	Papal States	Papal States
112	1860	Italy	Sicily	Sicily
113	1860	Italy	Modena	Modena
114	1860	Italy	Parma	Parma
115	1860	Italy	Tuscany	Tuscany
116	1860	Russia	China	China
117	1861	United Kingdom	none	S. Nigeria
118	1861	United Kingdom	none	Mozambique
119	1861	France	Monaco	Monaco
120	1861	Spain	Dominican Rep.	Dominican Rep.
121	1862	United Kingdom	Bahrein	Bahrein
122	1862	France	none	Djibouti
123	1862	France	Vietnam	Cochin China
124	1863	United States	Honduras	Honduras
125	1863	France	none	Benin
126	1863	France	Cambodia	Cambodia
127	1864	France	none	New Caledonia
128	1864	Prussia	Denmark	Denmark
129	1864	Prussia	Denmark	Denmark
130	1864	Austria-Hungary	Denmark	Denmark
131	1864	Greece	United Kingdom	Ionian Is.
132	1864	Russia	none	Russia
133	1865	Dominican Rep.	Spain	Dominican Rep.
134	1865	United Kingdom	Bhutan	Bhutan
135	1866	Chile	Bolivia	Chile
136	1866	Prussia	Hanover	Hanover
137	1866	Prussia	Frankfort	Frankfort
138	1866	Prussia	Nassau	Nassau
139	1866	Prussia	Hesse Elec.	Hesse Elec.
140	1866	Prussia	Austria-Hungary	Austria-Hungary
141	1866	Italy	Austria-Hungary	Austria-Hungary
142	1867	United States	none	Midway Is.
143	1867	United States	Russia	Alaska
144	1867	Brazil	Bolivia	Bolivia
145	1867	Luxembourg	Netherlands	Luxembourg
146	1867	France	Vietnam	Cochin China
147	1867	Germany	Oldenburg	Oldenburg
148	1867	Germany	Anhalt/Dessau	Anhalt/Dessau
149	1867	Germany	Brunswick	Brunswick
150	1867	Germany	Bremen	Bremen
151	1867	Germany	Hamburg	Hamburg
152	1867	Germany	Lippe	Lippe
153	1867	Germany	Mecklenburg S.	Mecklenburg S.
154	1867	Germany	Saxe/Meiningen	Saxe/Meiningen
155	1867	Germany	Waldeck	Waldeck
156	1867	Germany	Saxony	Saxony
157	1867	Germany	Lubeck	Lubeck

Appendix

Case #	Year	Gaining Side	Losing Side	Unit Exchanged
158	1867	Germany	Hesse G.D.	Hesse G.D.
159	1867	Germany	Mecklenburg	Mecklenburg
160	1867	Thailand	France	Cambodia
161	1868	United Kingdom	Lesotho	Lesotho
162	1868	Russia	Bukhara	Bukhara
163	1869	United Kingdom	none	India
164	1869	Italy	none	Eritrea
165	1870	Brazil	Paraguay	Paraguay
166	1870	Argentina	Paraguay	Paraguay
167	1870	France	none	Algeria
168	1870	Italy	Papal States	Papal States
169	1871	United Kingdom	none	South Africa
170	1871	United Kingdom	Netherlands	Ghana
171	1871	Germany	France	France
172	1871	Germany	Bavaria	Bavaria
173	1871	Germany	Baden	Baden
174	1871	Germany	Wurttemburg	Wurttemburg
175	1871	Russia	China	China
176	1871	Ottoman Empire	Asir	Asir
177	1872	United States	United Kingdom	Canada
178	1872	Ottoman Empire	Yemen	Yemen
179	1872	Ottoman Empire	Qatar	Qatar
180	1873	Russia	none	Russia
181	1873	Russia	Kiva	Kiva
182	1873	Japan	none	Japan
183	1874	United Kingdom	none	Malay States
184	1874	United Kingdom	Fiji	Fiji
185	1874	France	Vietnam	Cochin China
186	1874	Egypt	none	Sudan
187	1875	Portugal	United Kingdom	Mozambique
188	1875	Russia	Japan	Japan
189	1875	Ottoman Empire	Al Hasa	Al Hasa
190	1875	Japan	Russia	Russia
191	1876	United Kingdom	Afghanistan	Afghanistan
192	1876	Russia	Kokand	Kokand
193	1877	United Kingdom	none	West Africa
194	1877	United Kingdom	none	Tokelau Is.
195	1877	United Kingdom	Transvaal	Transvaal
196	1878	Paraguay	Argentina	Argentina
197	1878	United Kingdom	none	South Africa
198	1878	United Kingdom	Ottoman Empire	Cyprus
199	1878	Austria-Hungary	Ottoman Empire	Bosnia
200	1878	Austria-Hungary	Ottoman Empire	Herzegovina
201	1878	Austria-Hungary	Ottoman Empire	Albania
202	1878	Serbia	Ottoman Empire	Serbia
203	1878	Serbia	Ottoman Empire	Ottoman Empire
204	1878	Montenegro	Ottoman Empire	Montenegro

Territorial Changes and International Conflict

Case #	Year	Gaining Side	Losing Side	Unit Exchanged
205	1878	Montenegro	Ottoman Empire	Ottoman Empire
206	1878	Romania	Ottoman Empire	Romania
207	1878	Romania	Ottoman Empire	Ottoman Empire
208	1878	Romania	Ottoman Empire	Ottoman Empire
209	1878	Russia	Romania	Romania
210	1878	Russia	Ottoman Empire	Ottoman Empire
211	1879	Argentina	none	Argentina
212	1879	Egypt	Ethiopia	Ethiopia
213	1880	France	none	Polynesia
214	1880	France	none	Congo
215	1880	Montenegro	Ottoman Empire	Ottoman Empire
216	1880	Transvaal	United Kingdom	Transvaal
217	1880	Ottoman Empire	Montenegro	Montenegro
218	1881	Chile	Argentina	Argentina
219	1881	Argentina	Chile	Chile
220	1881	France	none	Polynesia
221	1881	France	Tunisia	Tunisia
222	1881	Greece	Ottoman Empire	Ottoman Empire
223	1881	Russia	none	Russia
224	1881	China	Russia	Russia
225	1882	United Kingdom	Egypt	Egypt
226	1883	Chile	Peru	Peru
227	1883	France	none	Benin
228	1883	France	Vietnam	Vietnam
229	1884	Chile	Bolivia	Bolivia
230	1884	United Kingdom	none	Natal
231	1884	United Kingdom	none	Papua
232	1884	United Kingdom	none	Somaliland
233	1884	United Kingdom	Transvaal	Transvaal
234	1884	France	none	Djibouti
235	1884	Germany	none	West Africa
236	1884	Germany	none	Togoland
237	1884	Germany	none	New Guinea
238	1884	Germany	none	Kamerun
239	1884	Ethiopia	Egypt	Ethiopia
240	1884	Sudan	United Kingdom	Sudan
241	1885	United Kingdom	none	Botswana
242	1885	United Kingdom	none	S. Nigeria
243	1885	United Kingdom	none	South Africa
244	1885	France	none	Gabon
245	1885	France	Malagasy	Malagasy
246	1885	Spain	none	Rio Muni
247	1885	Spain	none	Spanish Sahara
248	1885	Portugal	Belgium	Zaire
249	1885	Germany	none	Ruanda-Burundi
250	1885	Germany	none	Pacific Trust
251	1885	Germany	none	Solomon Is.

Appendix

Case #	Year	Gaining Side	Losing Side	Unit Exchanged
252	1885	Germany	none	Kenya
253	1885	Italy	none	Eritrea
254	1885	Russia	none	Russia
255	1886	United Kingdom	none	Aden Prot.
256	1886	United Kingdom	Burma	Burma
257	1886	France	none	Comoros
258	1886	Portugal	Zanzibar	Mozambique
259	1887	United Kingdom	none	South Africa
260	1887	United Kingdom	none	New Hebrides
261	1887	United Kingdom	none	New Zealand
262	1887	United Kingdom	Zanzibar	Kenya
263	1887	United Kingdom	Maldive Is.	Maldive Is.
264	1887	France	none	New Hebrides
265	1887	France	none	Wallis/Futuna
266	1888	Chile	none	Easter Is.
267	1888	United Kingdom	none	N. Borneo
268	1888	United Kingdom	none	Christmas Is.
269	1888	United Kingdom	none	Cook Is.
270	1888	United Kingdom	none	Sarawak
271	1888	United Kingdom	none	Malay States
272	1888	United Kingdom	Brunei	Brunei
273	1888	France	none	West Africa
274	1888	France	none	Wallis/Futuna
275	1888	Germany	none	Nauru
276	1888	Germany	Zanzibar	Tanzania
277	1889	United Kingdom	none	Malawi
278	1889	United Kingdom	none	Gambia
279	1889	United Kingdom	Zanzibar	Somalia
280	1889	United Kingdom	Malay States	Malay States
281	1889	France	none	Ivory Coast
282	1889	Italy	none	Eritrea
283	1889	Italy	Zanzibar	Somalia
284	1890	United Kingdom	none	Kenya
285	1890	United Kingdom	Germany	Kenya
286	1890	United Kingdom	Zanzibar	Zanzibar
287	1890	United Kingdom	Swaziland	Swaziland
288	1890	United Kingdom	Sikkim	Sikkim
289	1890	Portugal	none	Angola
290	1890	Germany	none	Tanzania
291	1890	Germany	United Kingdom	Heligoland
292	1890	Germany	United Kingdom	West Africa
293	1891	United Kingdom	none	Zambia
294	1891	Belgium	Portugal	Angola
295	1891	Portugal	Belgium	Zaire
296	1892	United Kingdom	none	Gilbert/Ellice
297	1892	United Kingdom	United Arab Emirates	United Arab Emirates

Case #	Year	Gaining Side	Losing Side	Unit Exchanged
298	1892	Italy	United Kingdom	Somalia
299	1893	United Kingdom	none	Solomon Is.
300	1893	United Kingdom	none	Zimbabwe
301	1893	United Kingdom	Afghanistan	Afghanistan
302	1893	France	none	West Africa
303	1893	France	none	Antarctica
304	1893	France	Laos	Laos
305	1893	Transvaal	United Kingdom	Swaziland
306	1894	United Kingdom	none	Uganda
307	1894	United Kingdom	none	South Africa
308	1894	France	none	Benin
309	1894	France	none	C. African Rep.
310	1894	France	Belgium	Zaire
311	1894	Italy	none	Sudan
312	1895	Brazil	Paraguay	Paraguay
313	1895	United Kingdom	none	South Africa
314	1895	Russia	Afghanistan	Afghanistan
315	1895	Japan	China	Taiwan
316	1896	United Kingdom	none	Ghana
317	1896	United Kingdom	none	Uganda
318	1896	United Kingdom	none	Ghana
319	1896	United Kingdom	none	Sierra Leone
320	1896	France	Malagasy	Malagasy
321	1897	Mexico	France	Clipperton Is.
322	1897	United Kingdom	none	Ghana
323	1897	United Kingdom	Italy	Sudan
324	1897	United Kingdom	Ethiopia	Ethiopia
325	1897	Ottoman Empire	Greece	Greece
326	1898	United States	none	Wake Is.
327	1898	United States	Hawaii	Hawaii
328	1898	United States	Spain	Guam
329	1898	United States	Spain	Philippines
330	1898	United States	Spain	Puerto Rico
331	1898	United States	Spain	Cuba
332	1898	United Kingdom	none	Solomon Is.
333	1898	United Kingdom	France	Nigeria
334	1898	United Kingdom	China	China
335	1898	United Kingdom	China	Hong Kong
336	1898	France	United Kingdom	West Africa
337	1898	Russia	China	China
338	1898	none	Ottoman Empire	Crete
339	1899	United States	Western Samoa	Samoa
340	1899	Venezuela	United Kingdom	Guyana
341	1899	United Kingdom	Venezuela	Venezuela
342	1899	United Kingdom	Germany	Togoland
343	1899	United Kingdom	Germany	Solomon Is.
344	1899	United Kingdom	Sudan	Sudan

Appendix

Case #	Year	Gaining Side	Losing Side	Unit Exchanged
345	1899	United Kingdom	Kuwait	Kuwait
346	1899	France	none	West Africa
347	1899	Germany	United Kingdom	Ghana
348	1899	Germany	Spain	Pacific Trust
349	1899	Germany	Western Samoa	Samoa
350	1900	United Kingdom	Tonga Is.	Tonga Is.
351	1900	Russia	China	Manchukuo
352	1902	Cuba	United States	Cuba
353	1902	Chile	Argentina	Argentina
354	1902	Argentina	Chile	Chile
355	1902	United Kingdom	Ethiopia	Ethiopia
356	1902	United Kingdom	Transvaal	Transvaal
357	1902	United Kingdom	Orange Free State	Orange Free State
358	1903	United States	Panama	Canal Zone
359	1903	United States	United Kingdom	Canada
360	1903	Panama	Colombia	Panama
361	1903	Brazil	Bolivia	Bolivia
362	1903	Bolivia	Brazil	Brazil
363	1903	United Kingdom	none	N. Nigeria
364	1903	France	Morocco	Morocco
365	1904	Brazil	Ecuador	Ecuador
366	1904	France	United Kingdom	Senegal
367	1904	France	United Kingdom	West Africa
368	1904	France	United Kingdom	Guinea
369	1904	France	Thailand	Thailand
370	1904	Thailand	France	Indochina
371	1905	Norway	Sweden	Norway
372	1905	China	Russia	Manchukuo
373	1905	Japan	Russia	China
374	1905	Japan	Russia	Russia
375	1905	Japan	Korea	Korea
376	1906	United Kingdom	Ottoman Empire	Israel
377	1906	Belgium	United Kingdom	Sudan
378	1907	Brazil	Colombia	Colombia
379	1907	Brazil	Bolivia	Bolivia
380	1907	Netherlands	none	Indonesia
381	1907	France	Morocco	Morocco
382	1907	France	Thailand	Thailand
383	1907	Thailand	France	Indochina
384	1908	Bulgaria	Ottoman Empire	Bulgaria
385	1909	Peru	Bolivia	Bolivia
386	1909	United Kingdom	Thailand	Malay States
387	1909	France	none	Mauritania
388	1910	United Kingdom	Belgium	Zaire
389	1910	United Kingdom	Bhutan	Bhutan
390	1910	Belgium	United Kingdom	Uganda
391	1910	Morocco	France	Morocco

Territorial Changes and International Conflict

Case #	Year	Gaining Side	Losing Side	Unit Exchanged
392	1911	United Kingdom	Liberia	Liberia
393	1911	France	none	Chad
394	1911	Germany	France	Ger. Cameroon
395	1911	Liberia	United Kingdom	Sierra Leone
396	1912	France	Morocco	Morocco
397	1912	Spain	Morocco	Morocco
398	1912	Italy	Ottoman Empire	Aegean Is.
399	1912	Italy	Ottoman Empire	Libya
400	1912	Albania	Ottoman Empire	Albania
401	1913	Serbia	Bulgaria	Bulgaria
402	1913	Serbia	Ottoman Empire	Ottoman Empire
403	1913	Montenegro	Ottoman Empire	Ottoman Empire
404	1913	Greece	Bulgaria	Bulgaria
405	1913	Greece	Ottoman Empire	Ottoman Empire
406	1913	Greece	Ottoman Empire	Ottoman Empire
407	1913	Greece	none	Crete
408	1913	Bulgaria	Ottoman Empire	Ottoman Empire
409	1913	Romania	Bulgaria	Bulgaria
410	1913	Saudi Arabia	Ottoman Empire	Al Hasa
411	1914	United Kingdom	Malay States	Malay States
412	1914	Italy	Albania	Albania
413	1914	Albania	Greece	Greece
414	1914	Asir	Ottoman Empire	Ottoman Empire
415	1914	Japan	Germany	China
416	1915	United Kingdom	Yemen	Yemen
417	1915	Qatar	Ottoman Empire	Ottoman Empire
418	1916	United States	Nicaragua	Nicaragua
419	1916	United Kingdom	Qatar	Qatar
420	1916	Spain	France	Morocco
421	1917	United States	Denmark	Virgin Is.
422	1917	Finland	Russia	Finland
423	1918	Poland	Soviet Union	Poland
424	1918	Czechoslovakia	Austria	Austria
425	1918	Estonia	Soviet Union	Estonia
426	1918	Latvia	Soviet Union	Latvia
427	1918	Lithuania	Soviet Union	Lithuania
428	1918	Ukraine	Soviet Union	Ukraine
429	1918	Armenia	Soviet Union	Armenia
430	1918	Georgia	Soviet Union	Georgia
431	1918	Azerbaijan	Soviet Union	Azerbaijan
432	1918	Yemen	Ottoman Empire	Yemen
433	1919	United Kingdom	Germany	Togoland
434	1919	United Kingdom	Germany	Ger. Cameroons
435	1919	Belgium	Germany	Germany
436	1919	Luxembourg	Germany	Germany
437	1919	France	Germany	Togo
438	1919	France	Germany	Cameroon

Appendix

Case #	Year	Gaining Side	Losing Side	Unit Exchanged
439	1919	France	Germany	Equat. Africa
440	1919	France	Germany	Saar
441	1919	France	Germany	Germany
442	1919	Portugal	Germany	Mozambique
443	1919	Poland	Germany	Germany
444	1919	Poland	Austria	Austria-Hungary
445	1919	Danzig	Germany	Germany
446	1919	Hungary	Austria	Hungary
447	1919	Italy	France	Tunisia
448	1919	Italy	Austria	Trieste
449	1919	Italy	Austria	Austria
450	1919	Serbia	Austria	Austria-Hungary
451	1919	Serbia	Bulgaria	Bulgaria
452	1919	Greece	Bulgaria	Bulgaria
453	1919	South Africa	Germany	West Africa
454	1919	Australia	Germany	Nauru
455	1920	Canada	United Kingdom	Canada
456	1920	Newfoundland	United Kingdom	Newfoundland
457	1920	United Kingdom	Germany	Tanzania
458	1920	United Kingdom	Turkey	Palestine
459	1920	United Kingdom	Turkey	Jordan
460	1920	United Kingdom	Turkey	Iraq
461	1920	France	Turkey	Syria
462	1920	Poland	Czechoslovakia	Czechoslovakia
463	1920	Poland	Lithuania	Lithuania
464	1920	Austria	Serbia	Serbia
465	1920	Czechoslovakia	Poland	Poland
466	1920	Czechoslovakia	Hungary	Hungary
467	1920	Italy	Serbia	Trieste
468	1920	Serbia	Hungary	Hungary
469	1920	Yugoslavia	Italy	Trieste
470	1920	Romania	Hungary	Hungary
471	1920	Romania	Soviet Union	Romania
472	1920	Soviet Union	Ukraine	Ukraine
473	1920	Soviet Union	Armenia	Armenia
474	1920	Soviet Union	Georgia	Georgia
475	1920	Soviet Union	Azerbaijan	Azerbaijan
476	1920	Denmark	Germany	Germany
477	1920	South Africa	United Kingdom	South Africa
478	1920	Hejaz Sultanate	Turkey	Hejaz Sultanate
479	1920	Japan	Germany	Pacific Trust
480	1920	Australia	United Kingdom	Australia
481	1920	Australia	Germany	New Guinea
482	1920	New Zealand	United Kingdom	New Zealand
483	1920	New Zealand	Germany	Samoa
484	1921	Costa Rica	Panama	Panama
485	1921	Poland	Soviet Union	Soviet Union

Case #	Year	Gaining Side	Losing Side	Unit Exchanged
486	1921	Hungary	Austria	Austria
487	1921	Soviet Union	Turkey	Turkey
488	1921	Finland	Sweden	Sweden
489	1921	Mongolia	China	Mongolia
490	1922	United States	none	Kingman Reef
491	1922	Colombia	Venezuela	Venezuela
492	1922	Ireland	United Kingdom	Ireland
493	1922	Germany	Poland	Germany
494	1922	Poland	Germany	Poland
495	1922	Egypt	United Kingdom	Egypt
496	1922	China	Japan	China
497	1923	Lithuania	none	Lithuania
498	1924	Belgium	Germany	Ruanda-Burundi
499	1924	Italy	United Kingdom	Kenya
500	1924	Italy	Serbia	Serbia
501	1924	Serbia	Italy	Italy
502	1924	none	France	Tangier
503	1925	Italy	Egypt	Egypt
504	1925	Egypt	Italy	Libya
505	1926	United Kingdom	Turkey	Iraq
506	1926	New Zealand	United Kingdom	Tokelau Is.
507	1927	Belgium	Portugal	Angola
508	1927	Portugal	Belgium	Zaire
509	1928	Netherlands	United States	Indonesia
510	1928	Norway	United Kingdom	Bouvet
511	1929	Peru	Chile	Chile
512	1929	Vatican City	Italy	Vatican City
513	1930	China	United Kingdom	China
514	1932	France	Mexico	Clipperton Is.
515	1932	Iraq	United Kingdom	Iraq
516	1932	Japan	China	Manchukuo
517	1933	United Kingdom	Newfoundland	Newfoundland
518	1933	Japan	China	China
519	1934	Colombia	Peru	Peru
520	1934	Italy	France	Sudan
521	1934	Saudi Arabia	Yemen	Yemen
522	1935	Paraguay	Bolivia	Bolivia
523	1935	Germany	France	Saar
524	1935	Italy	France	Djibouti
525	1936	Italy	Ethiopia	Ethiopia
526	1937	Japan	China	China
527	1938	Germany	Austria	Austria
528	1938	Germany	Czechoslovakia	Czechoslovakia
529	1938	Poland	Czechoslovakia	Czechoslovakia
530	1938	Hungary	Czechoslovakia	Slovakia
531	1939	Germany	Czechoslovakia	Czechoslovakia
532	1939	Germany	Lithuania	Lithuania

Appendix

Case #	Year	Gaining Side	Losing Side	Unit Exchanged
533	1939	Hungary	Czechoslovakia	Czechoslovakia
534	1939	Slovakia	Czechoslovakia	Czechoslovakia
535	1939	Italy	Albania	Albania
536	1939	Lithuania	Soviet Union	Poland
537	1939	Turkey	France	Syria
538	1940	Bulgaria	Romania	Romania
539	1940	Soviet Union	Estonia	Estonia
540	1940	Soviet Union	Latvia	Latvia
541	1940	Soviet Union	Lithuania	Lithuania
542	1941	Ethiopia	Italy	Ethiopia
543	1942	Peru	Ecuador	Ecuador
544	1944	Iceland	Denmark	Iceland
545	1945	United States	Japan	Ryukyu Is.
546	1945	Poland	Germany	Germany
547	1945	Czechoslovakia	Germany	Czechoslovakia
548	1945	Czechoslovakia	Hungary	Czechoslovakia
549	1945	Czechoslovakia	Slovakia	Slovakia
550	1945	Albania	Italy	Albania
551	1945	Soviet Union	Germany	Soviet Union
552	1945	Soviet Union	Poland	Poland
553	1945	Soviet Union	Czechoslovakia	Czechoslovakia
554	1945	Soviet Union	Japan	Japan
555	1945	China	Japan	Taiwan
556	1945	China	Japan	China
557	1945	none	Germany	Austria
558	1945	none	Germany	Germany
559	1945	none	Japan	Korea
560	1945	none	Japan	Japan
561	1946	Syria	France	Syria
562	1946	Lebanon	France	Lebanon
563	1946	Jordan	United Kingdom	Jordan
564	1946	Philippines	United States	Philippines
565	1947	United States	Japan	Pacific Trust
566	1947	France	W. Germany	Saar
567	1947	France	Italy	Italy
568	1947	Czechoslovakia	Hungary	Hungary
569	1947	Albania	Italy	Albania
570	1947	Yugoslavia	Italy	Italy
571	1947	Greece	Italy	Aegean Is.
572	1947	Soviet Union	Romania	Romania
573	1947	Soviet Union	Finland	Finland
574	1947	South Africa	none	South Africa
575	1947	India	United Kingdom	India
576	1947	Pakistan	United Kingdom	Pakistan
577	1947	Australia	United Kingdom	Heard-McDonald
578	1947	none	Italy	Libya
579	1947	none	Italy	Trieste

Territorial Changes and International Conflict

Case #	Year	Gaining Side	Losing Side	Unit Exchanged
580	1947	none	Italy	Somalia
581	1947	none	Italy	Eritrea
582	1947	Canada	United Kingdom	Newfoundland
583	1948	Israel	United Kingdom	Israel
584	1948	N. Korea	Soviet Union	N. Korea
585	1948	S. Korea	United States	S. Korea
586	1948	Burma	United Kingdom	Burma
587	1948	Sri Lanka	United Kingdom	Sri Lanka
588	1949	Netherlands	W. Germany	W. Germany
589	1949	Belgium	W. Germany	W. Germany
590	1949	Luxembourg	W. Germany	W. Germany
591	1949	France	W. Germany	W. Germany
592	1949	Italy	none	Somalia
593	1949	Egypt	Israel	Israel
594	1949	Jordan	Israel	Israel
595	1949	Taiwan	China	Taiwan
596	1949	India	Pakistan	Kashmir
597	1949	Bhutan	India	India
598	1949	Bhutan	India	Bhutan
599	1949	Pakistan	India	Kashmir
600	1949	Indonesia	Netherlands	Indonesia
601	1950	India	France	India
602	1950	India	Sikkim	Sikkim
603	1951	Poland	Soviet Union	Soviet Union
604	1951	Soviet Union	Poland	Poland
605	1951	Libya	none	Libya
606	1952	Ethiopia	none	Eritrea
607	1952	Japan	none	Japan
608	1953	Japan	United States	Ryukyu Is.
609	1953	Cambodia	France	Cambodia
610	1954	E. Germany	Soviet Union	E. Germany
611	1954	Italy	none	Trieste
612	1954	Yugoslavia	none	Trieste
613	1954	India	France	India
614	1954	Laos	France	Laos
615	1954	N. Vietnam	France	N. Vietnam
616	1954	S. Vietnam	France	S. Vietnam
617	1955	France	Libya	Libya
618	1955	W. Germany	none	W. Germany
619	1955	Austria	none	Austria
620	1955	China	Taiwan	Taiwan
621	1955	Australia	United Kingdom	Cocos Is.
622	1956	W. Germany	Belgium	Belgium
623	1956	Morocco	France	Morocco
624	1956	Morocco	Spain	W. Sahara
625	1956	Morocco	none	Tangier
626	1956	Tunisia	France	Tunisia

Appendix

Case #	Year	Gaining Side	Losing Side	Unit Exchanged
627	1956	Sudan	United Kingdom	Sudan
628	1956	Egypt	United Kingdom	Egypt
629	1956	Japan	Soviet Union	Soviet Union
630	1957	W. Germany	France	Saar
631	1957	Ghana	United Kingdom	Ghana
632	1957	Ghana	United Kingdom	Togoland
633	1957	Malaysia	United Kingdom	Malaysia
634	1958	Guinea	France	Guinea
635	1958	Morocco	Spain	W. Sahara
636	1958	Egypt	Syria	Syria
637	1958	India	Pakistan	Pakistan
638	1958	Pakistan	Oman	Oman
639	1958	Pakistan	India	India
640	1958	Australia	United Kingdom	Christmas Is.
641	1960	Honduras	Nicaragua	Nicaragua
642	1960	Cyprus	United Kingdom	Cyprus
643	1960	Mali	France	Mali
644	1960	Senegal	Mali	Senegal
645	1960	Benin	France	Benin
646	1960	Mauritania	France	Mauritania
647	1960	Niger	France	Niger
648	1960	Ivory Coast	France	Ivory Coast
649	1960	Upper Volta	France	Upper Volta
650	1960	Togo	France	Togo
651	1960	Cameroun	France	Cameroun
652	1960	Nigeria	United Kingdom	Nigeria
653	1960	Gabon	France	Gabon
654	1960	C. African Rep.	France	C. African Rep.
655	1960	Chad	France	Chad
656	1960	Congo Braz.	France	Congo Braz.
657	1960	Zaire	Belgium	Zaire
658	1960	Somalia	United Kingdom	Somaliland
659	1960	Somalia	Italy	Somalia
660	1960	Malagasy	France	Malagasy
661	1961	Benin	Portugal	Benin
662	1961	Sierra Leone	United Kingdom	Sierra Leone
663	1961	Cameroun	United Kingdom	Cameroons
664	1961	Nigeria	United Kingdom	Cameroons
665	1961	Tanzania	United Kingdom	Tanzania
666	1961	Syria	United Arab Rep.	Syria
667	1961	Kuwait	United Kingdom	Kuwait
668	1961	China	Burma	Burma
669	1961	India	Portugal	India
670	1961	Nepal	China	Nepal
671	1962	Jamaica	United Kingdom	Jamaica
672	1962	Trinidad	United Kingdom	Trinidad
673	1962	Uganda	United Kingdom	Uganda

Territorial Changes and International Conflict

Case #	Year	Gaining Side	Losing Side	Unit Exchanged
674	1962	Burundi	Belgium	Burundi
675	1962	Rwanda	Belgium	Rwanda
676	1962	Algeria	France	Algeria
677	1962	Western Samoa	New Zealand	Western Samoa
678	1963	Mexico	United States	Mexico
679	1963	W. Germany	Netherlands	W. Germany
680	1963	Kenya	United Kingdom	Kenya
681	1963	Zanzibar	United Kingdom	Zanzibar
682	1963	Pakistan	China	Pakistan
683	1963	Malaysia	United Kingdom	Singapore
684	1963	Malaysia	United Kingdom	N. Borneo
685	1963	Malaysia	United Kingdom	Sarawak
686	1963	Indonesia	Netherlands	West Irian
687	1964	Malta	United Kingdom	Malta
688	1964	Tanzania	Zanzibar	Zanzibar
689	1964	Zambia	United Kingdom	Zambia
690	1964	Malawi	United Kingdom	Malawi
691	1965	Gambia	United Kingdom	Gambia
692	1965	Jordan	Saudi Arabia	Saudi Arabia
693	1965	Saudi Arabia	Jordan	Jordan
694	1965	Maldive Is.	United Kingdom	Maldive Is.
695	1965	Singapore	Malaysia	Singapore
696	1966	Barbados	United Kingdom	Barbados
697	1966	Guyana	United Kingdom	Guyana
698	1966	Lesotho	United Kingdom	Lesotho
699	1966	Botswana	United Kingdom	Botswana
700	1967	Israel	Egypt	Egypt
701	1967	Israel	Syria	Syria
702	1967	Israel	Jordan	Jordan
703	1967	Yemen	United Kingdom	Yemen
704	1967	Oman	United Kingdom	Oman
705	1968	Equat. Guinea	Spain	Equat. Guinea
706	1968	Swaziland	United Kingdom	Swaziland
707	1968	Mauritius	United Kingdom	Mauritius
708	1968	Japan	United States	Pacific Is.
709	1968	India	Pakistan	Pakistan
710	1968	Pakistan	India	India
711	1968	Nauru	Australia	Nauru
712	1969	Morocco	Spain	Ifni
713	1969	Saudi Arabia	Kuwait	Kuwait
714	1969	Kuwait	Saudi Arabia	Saudi Arabia
715	1970	Fiji	United Kingdom	Fiji
716	1970	Tonga Is.	United Kingdom	Tonga Is.
717	1971	Nicaragua	United States	Nicaragua
718	1971	Iran	U. Arab Emirate	U. Arab Emirate
719	1971	Iran	U. Arab Emirate	U. Arab Emirate
720	1971	Bahrein	United Kingdom	Bahrein

Appendix

Case #	Year	Gaining Side	Losing Side	Unit Exchanged
721	1971	Qatar	United Kingdom	Qatar
722	1971	Trucial Oman	United Kingdom	Trucial Oman
723	1971	Trucial Oman	U. Arab Emirate	U. Arab Emirate
724	1971	India	Pakistan	Pakistan
725	1971	Pakistan	India	India
726	1971	Bangladesh	Pakistan	Bangladesh
727	1972	Honduras	United States	Honduras
728	1972	N. Yemen	Yemen	Yemen
729	1972	Trucial Oman	U. Arab Emirate	U. Arab Emirate
730	1972	Japan	United States	Ryukyu Is.
731	1972	India	Pakistan	India
732	1972	Pakistan	India	Pakistan
733	1973	Bahamas	United Kingdom	Bahamas
734	1973	Libya	Chad	Chad
735	1973	Israel	Syria	Syria
736	1974	Grenada	United Kingdom	Grenada
737	1974	Guinea-Bissau	Portugal	Guinea-Bissau
738	1974	Turkey	Cyprus	Cyprus
739	1974	Egypt	Israel	Egypt
740	1974	Sri Lanka	India	India
741	1975	Suriname	Netherlands	Suriname
742	1975	Cape Verde	Portugal	Cape Verde
743	1975	Sao Tome Princ.	Portugal	Sao Tome Princ.
744	1975	Angola	Portugal	Angola
745	1975	Mozambique	Portugal	Mozambique
746	1975	Comoros	France	Comoros
747	1975	Iraq	Saudi Arabia	Saudi Arabia
748	1975	Egypt	Israel	Egypt
749	1975	Saudi Arabia	Iraq	Iraq
750	1975	N. Vietnam	S. Vietnam	S. Vietnam
751	1975	Papua N. Guinea	Australia	Papua N. Guinea
752	1976	France	Comoros	Mayotte
753	1976	Mauritania	Spain	Sahara
754	1976	Seychelles	United Kingdom	Seychelles
755	1976	Seychelles	United Kingdom	Ind. Oc. Terr.
756	1976	Morocco	Spain	W. Sahara
757	1976	Syria	Israel	Syria
758	1976	Indonesia	Portugal	Timor
759	1977	Djibouti	France	Djibouti
760	1978	Dominica	United Kingdom	Dominica
761	1978	Panama	United States	Canal Zone
762	1978	Solomon Is.	United States	Solomon Is.
763	1978	Tuvalu	United Kingdom	Tuvalu
764	1979	St. Lucia	United Kingdom	St. Lucia
765	1979	St. Vincent	United Kingdom	St. Vincent
766	1979	Egypt	Israel	Egypt
767	1979	Kiribati	United Kingdom	Kiribati

Case #	Year	Gaining Side	Losing Side	Unit Exchanged
768	1980	Zimbabwe	United Kingdom	Zimbabwe
769	1980	Morocco	Mauritania	Mauritania
770	1980	Vanuatu	France	Vanuatu

BIBLIOGRAPHY

Akehurst, Michael. 1982. *A Modern Introduction to International Law*. 4th edition. London: Allen and Unwin.

Alcock, Norman. 1972. *The War Disease*. Oakville, Ontario: CPRI Press.

Aldrich, John, and Forrest, Nelson. 1984. *Linear Probability, Logit, and Probit Models*. Sage University Paper Series on Quantitative Applications in the Social Sciences, nos. 07–045. Beverly Hills: Sage Publications.

Allan, Pierre. 1983. *Crisis Bargaining and the Arms Race: A Theoretical Model*. Cambridge, Mass.: Ballinger Publishing.

Axelrod, Robert. 1986. "An Evolutionary Approach to Norms." *American Political Science Review*, 80:1095–1111.

Bairoch, Paul. 1974. "Europe's GNP, 1800–1970." *Journal of European Economic History*, 3:557–608.

Ball, Desmond. 1985. "Modern Technology and Geopolitics." In *On Geopolitics: Classic and Nuclear*, eds. Curo Zoppo and Charles Zorgbibe. Dordecht, The Netherlands: Martinus Nijhoff.

Bercovitch, J. 1965. "Third Parties in Conflict Management: The Structure and Conditions of Effective Mediation in International Relations." *International Journal*, 40:736–752.

Betts, Raymond. 1985. *Uncertain Dimensions: Western Overseas Empires in the 20th Century*. Minneapolis: University of Minnesota Press.

Boggs, S. Whittemore. 1940. *International Boundaries: A Study of Boundary Functions and Problems*. New York: Columbia University Press.

Boulding, Kenneth. 1962. *Conflict and Defense*. New York: Harper and Row.

Bremer, Stuart. 1982. "The Contagiousness of Coercion: The Spread of Serious International Disputes, 1900–1976." *International Interactions*, 9:29–55.

———. 1980. "National Capabilities and War Proneness." In *The Correlates of War II: Testing Some Realpolitik Models*, ed. J. David Singer. New York: Free Press.

Bueno de Mesquita, Bruce. 1981. *The War Trap*. New Haven: Yale University Press.

Bull, Hedley. 1977. *The Anarchical Society*. London: Macmillan.

Choucri, Nazli, and Robert North. 1975. *Nations in Conflict*. San Francisco: W.H. Freeman.

Davis, William, George Duncan, and Randolph Siverson. 1978. "The Dynamics of Warfare." *American Journal of Political Science*, 22:772–792.

Day, Alan, ed. 1987. *Border and Territorial Disputes*. 2nd ed. Essex: Longman.

Deutsch, Karl, and J. David Singer. 1964. "Multipolar Power Systems and International Stability." *World Politics*, 16:390–406.

Diehl, Paul. 1985. "Arms Races to War: Testing Some Empirical Linkages." *Sociological Quarterly*, 26:331–349.

———. 1985. "Contiguity and Military Escalation in Major Power Rivalries, 1816–1980." *Journal of Politics*, 47:1203–1211.

Diehl, Paul, and Gary Goertz. 1988. "Territorial Changes and Militarized Conflict." *Journal of Conflict Resolution*, 32:103–122.

Doran, Charles, and Wes Parsons. 1980. "War and the Cycle of Relative Power." *American Political Science Review*, 74:947–965.

Duchacek, Ivo. 1986. *The Territorial Dimension of Politics: Within, Among, and Across Nations*. Boulder: Westview Press.

Dunnigan, James, and Austin Bay. 1986. *A Quick and Dirty Guide to War*. Revised edition. New York: William Morrow.

Elias, Norbert. 1952. *Power and Civility*. New York: Pantheon.

Eyestone, Robert. 1977. "Confusion, Diffusion, and Innovation." *American Political Science Review*, 71:441–447.

Faber, Jan, Henk Houweling, and Jan Siccama. 1984. "Diffusion of War: Some Theoretical Considerations and Empirical Evidence." *Journal of Peace Research*, 21:277–288.

Ferris, Wayne. 1974. *The Power Capabilities of Nation-States*. Lexington, Mass.: Lexington Books.

Garnham, David. 1976. "Dyadic International War, 1816–1965: The Role of Power Parity and Geographic Proximity." *Western Political Quarterly*, 27:97–120.

Glassner, Martin, and Harm de Blij. 1989. *Systematic Political Geography*. 4th ed. New York: John Wiley.

Gochman, Charles. 1990. "Interstate Metrics: Conceptualizing, Operationalizing, and Measuring the Geographic Proximity of States Since the Congress of Vienna." *International Interactions* (forthcoming).

———, and Zeev Maoz. 1984. "Militarized Interstate Disputes, 1816–1976: Procedures, Patterns, and Insights." *Journal of Conflict Resolution*, 29:585–616.

Gray, Colin. 1977. *The Geopolitics of the Nuclear Era: Heartland, Rimland, and the Technological Revolution*. New York: Crane, Russak, and Co.

Gray, Virginia. 1973. "Innovation in the States: A Diffusion Study." *American Political Science Review*, 67:1174–1185.

Hayduk, Leslie. 1987. *Structural Equation Modeling with LISREL: Essentials and Advances*. Baltimore: Johns Hopkins University Press.

Holdich, Thomas. 1916. *Political Frontiers and Boundary Making*. London: Macmillan.

Houweling, Henk, and Jan Siccama. 1985. "The Epidemiology of War, 1960–1980." *Journal of Conflict Resolution*, 29:641–663.
Jacobson, Harold. 1962. "The United Nations and Colonialism." *International Organization*, 16:37–56.
Kaplan, Morton. 1957. *System and Process in International Politics*. New York: John Wiley.
Kelly, Philip. 1986. "Escalation of Regional Conflict: Testing the Shatterbelt Concept." *Political Geography Quarterly*, 5:161–180.
Kende, Istvan. 1971. "Twenty-five Years of Local Wars." *Journal of Peace Research*, 2:5–22.
Kennedy, Paul. 1987. *The Rise and Fall of the Great Powers*. New York: Random House.
Kirby, Andrew. 1985. "Pseudo-Random Thoughts on Space, Scale, and Ideology in Political Geography." *Political Geography Quarterly*, 4:5–18.
———, and Michael Ward. 1987. "The Spatial Analysis of Peace and War." *Comparative Political Studies*, 20:293–313.
———. 1987. "Space, Spatiality, Geography, Territoriality, Context, Locale, and Conflict." Paper presented at the roundtable on geopolitics at the annual meeting of the American Political Science Association, Chicago.
Koch, Howard, Robert North, and Dina Zinnes. 1960. "Some Theoretical Notes on Geography and International Conflict." *Journal of Conflict Resolution*, 4:4–14.
Krasner, Stephen, ed. 1982. *International Regimes*. Ithaca, New York: Cornell University Press.
Kratochwil, Friedrich. 1986. "Of Systems, Boundaries, and Territoriality: An Inquiry Into the Formation of the State System." *World Politics*, 39:27–52.
———, Paul Rohrlich, and Harpreet Mahajan. 1985. *Peace and Disputed Sovereignty: Reflections on Conflict Over Territory*. Latham, Maryland: University Press of America.
Leng, Russell. 1983. "When Will They Ever Learn: Coercive Bargaining in Recurrent Crises." *Journal of Conflict Resolution*, 27:379–419.
Lenin, V.I. 1939. *Imperialism: The Highest Stage of Capitalism*. New York: International Publishers.
Levy, Jack, and T. Clifton Morgan. 1986. "The War Weariness Hypothesis: An Empirical Test." *American Journal of Political Science*, 30:26–50.
Long, J. Scott. 1985. *Confirmatory Factor Analysis*. Sage University Paper Series on Quantitative Applications in the Social Sciences, nos. 07–033. Beverly Hills: Sage Publications.
Luard, Evan. 1970. "Frontier Disputes in Modern International Relations." In *International Regulation of Frontier Disputes*, ed. Evan Luard. New York: Praeger.

Mackinder, Halford. 1919. *Democratic Ideals and Reality.* New York: Henry Holt.
Malhotra, Maresh. 1983. "A Comparison of the Predictive Validity of Procedures for Analyzing Binary Data." *Journal of Business and Economic Statistics,* 1:326–336.
Mandel, Robert. 1980. "Roots of Modern Interstate Border Disputes." *Journal of Conflict Resolution,* 24:427–454.
Maoz, Zeev. 1989. "Joining the Club of Nations: Political Development and International Conflict, 1816–1976." *International Studies Quarterly,* 33:199–231.
———. 1989. "Power, Capabilities, and Paradoxical Conflict Outcomes." *World Politics,* 41:239–266.
McKinlay, Robert, and Richard Little. 1979. "The United States Aid Relationship: A Test of the Recipient Need and the Donor Interest Models." *Political Studies,* 27:236–250.
Midlarsky, Manus, ed. 1989. *Handbook of War Studies.* Winchester, Mass.: Unwin-Hyman.
———. 1975. *On War.* New York: Free Press.
———. 1970. "Mathematical Models of Instability and a Theory of Diffusion." *International Studies Quarterly,* 14:60–81.
Modelski, George. 1978. "The Long Cycle of Global Politics and the Nation-State." *Comparative Studies in Society and History,* 20:214–235.
Morgenthau, Hans. 1960. *Politics Among Nations.* 3rd ed. New York: Alfred Knopf.
Most, Benjamin, and Harvey Starr. 1989. *Inquiry, Logic and International Politics.* Columbia, S.C.: University of South Carolina Press.
———. 1980. "Diffusion, Reinforcement, Geopolitics, and the Spread of War." *American Political Science Review,* 74:932–946.
Most, Benjamin, Randolph Siverson, and Harvey Starr. 1989. "The Logic and Study of the Diffusion of International War." In *Handbook of War Studies,* ed. Manus Midlarsky. Winchester, Mass.: Unwin-Hyman.
Most, Benjamin, Philip Schrodt, Randolph Siverson, and Harvey Starr. 1990. "Border and Alliance Effects in the Diffusion of Major Power Conflict, 1815–1965." In *Prisoners of War?: Nation-States in the Modern Era,* eds. Charles Gochman and Alan Sabrosky. Lexington, Mass.: Lexington Books.
Mueller, John. 1989. *Retreat From Doomsday: The Obsolescence of Major War.* New York: Basic Books.
New York Times. November 13, 1989.
Nordquist, Kjell-Ake. 1986. "The Settlement of Border Conflicts: A Theoretical Model With Empirical Illustrations." Paper presented at the annual IPRA Conference, Sussex, England.
Northedge, F. S., and M. Dovelan. 1971. *International Disputes: The Political Aspects.* New York: St. Martin's Press.
Odell, John. 1979. "Correlates of United States Military Assistance and

Bibliography

Military Intervention." In *Testing Theories of Economic Imperialism*, eds. Steven Raosen and James Kurth. Lexington, Mass.: D.C. Heath and Co.

O'Connell, Robert. 1989. *Of Arms and Men: A History of War, Weapons, and Aggression*. New York: Oxford University Press.

O'Loughlin, John. 1987. "The Contribution of Political Geography to the Study of International Conflicts: A Research Agenda." Paper presented at the roundtable on geopolitics at the annual meeting of the American Political Science Association, Chicago.

———. 1987. "In the Spirit of Cooperation, Not Conflict: A Reply to Ward and Kirby." *Annals of the Association of American Geographers*, 77:284–288.

Organski, A.F.K. 1968. *World Politics*. 2nd ed. New York: Alfred Knopf.

Pearson, Frederic. 1974. "Geographic Proximity and Foreign Military Intervention." *Journal of Conflict Resolution*, 18:432–460.

Prescott, J.R.V. 1965. *The Geography of Frontiers and Boundaries*. Chicago: Aldine Publishing.

———. 1972. *Political Geography*. London: Methuen.

Ray, James Lee. 1987. *Global Politics*. 3rd ed. Boston: Houghton-Mifflin.

———. and Ayse Vural. 1986. "Power Disparities and Paradoxical Conflict Outcomes." *International Interactions*, 12:315–342.

Rejai, Mostafa, and Cynthia Enloe. 1981. "Nation-States and State-Nations." In *Perspectives on World Politics*, eds. Michael Smith, Richard Little, and Michael Shackleton. Chatham, N.J.: Chatham House.

Richardson, Lewis. 1960. *Statistics of Deadly Quarrels*. Pittsburgh: Boxwood Press.

Rosen, Steven. 1979. "The Open Door Imperative and U. S. Foreign Policy." In *Testing Theories of Economic Imperialism*, eds. Steven Rosen and James Kurth. Lexington, Mass.: D.C. Heath and Co.

Rosenau, James. 1988. "Patterned Chaos in Global Life: Structure and Process in the Two Worlds of World Politics." *International Political Science Review*, 9:327–364.

———. 1988. "The State in an Era of Cascading Politics: Wavering Concept, Widening Competence, Withering Colossus, or Weathering Change?" *Comparative Political Studies*, 21:13–44.

———. 1984. "A Pre-Theory Revisited: World Politics in an Era of Cascading Interdependence." *International Studies Quarterly*, 28:245–305.

Ross, Marc, and Elizabeth Homer. 1976. "Galton's Problem in Cross-National Research." *World Politics* 29:1–28.

Russett, Bruce, ed. 1972. *Peace, War, and Numbers*. Beverly Hills: Sage Publications.

———. 1972. "A Macroscopic View of International Politics." In *The Analysis of International Politics*, eds. James Rosenau, Vincent Davis, and Maurice East. New York: Free Press.

Schaefer, Philip, Gary Goertz, and Paul F. Diehl. 1990. "Territorial Change Coding Manual." Ann Arbor, Mich.: Correlates of War Project mimeo.

Schrodt, Philip. 1981. "Conflict as a Determinant of Territory." *Behavioral Science*, 26:37–50.

Schumpeter, Joseph. 1964. *History of Economic Analysis*. New York: Oxford University Press.

Schwernez, Karl de. 1983. *The Rise and Fall of British India*. New York: Methuen.

Sharma, Surya. 1976. *International Boundary Disputes and International Law*. Bombay: Tripathi.

Shaw, Malcolm. 1986. *Title to Territory in Africa*. Oxford: Clarendon Press.

Simon, Julian. 1989. "Lebensraum: Paradoxically, Population Growth May Eventually End Wars." *Journal of Conflict Resolution*, 33:164–180.

Singer, J. David, ed. 1980. *The Correlates of War II: Testing Some Realpolitik Models*. New York: Free Press.

———, and Thomas Cusack. 1981. "Periodicity, Inexorability, and Steermanship in International War." In *From National Development to Global Community: Essays in Honor of Karl Deutsch*, eds. Richard Merritt and Bruce Russett. London: Allen and Unwin.

Singer, J. David, Stuart Bremer, and John Stuckey. 1972. "Capability Distribution, Uncertainty, and Major Power War, 1820–1965." In *Peace, War and Numbers*, ed. Bruce Russett. Beverly Hills: Sage Publications.

Siverson, Randolph, and Harvey Starr. 1990. "Opportunity, Willingness, and the Diffusion of War, 1816–1965." *American Political Science Review*, 84:47–68.

Siverson, Randolph, and Michael Sullivan. 1983. "The Distribution of Power and the Onset of War." *Journal of Conflict Resolution*, 27:473–494.

Small, Melvin, and J. David Singer. 1982. *Resort to Arms*. Beverly Hills: Sage Publications.

Smith, Tony. 1981. *The Pattern of Imperialism: The United States, Great Britain, and the Late-Industrializing World Since 1815*. Cambridge: Cambridge University Press.

Sprout, Harold. 1963. "Geopolitical Hypotheses in Technological Perspective." *World Politics*, 15:187–212.

———, and Margaret Sprout. 1965. *The Ecological Perspective on Human Affairs*. Princeton: Princeton University Press.

Spykman, Nicholas. 1944. *The Geography of Peace*. New York: Harcourt Brace.

———. 1938. "Geography and Foreign Policy, I." *American Political Science Review*, 32:28–50.

Starr, Harvey. 1987. "Opportunity, Borders, and the Diffusion of

International Conflict: An Overview and Some Observations." Paper presented at the roundtable on geopolitics at the annual meeting of the American Political Science Association, Chicago.

———. 1975. *Coalitions and Future War: A Dyadic Study of Cooperation and Conflict.* Sage Professional Papers in International Studies, v.3. Beverly Hills: Sage Publications.

———. 1978. "Opportunity and Willingness, as Ordering Concepts in the Study of War." *International Interactions,* 4:363–387.

———, and Benjamin Most. 1985. "The Forms and Processes of War Diffusion: Research Update on Contagion in African Conflict." *Comparative Political Studies,* 18:206–227.

———. 1983. "Contagion and Border Effects on Contemporary African Conflict." *Comparative Political Studies,* 16:92–117.

———. 1978. "A Return Journey: Richardson, Frontiers and Wars in the 1946–65 Era." *Journal of Conflict Resolution,* 22:441–467.

———. 1976. "The Substance and Study of Borders in International Relations Research." *International Studies Quarterly,* 20:581–620.

Stoll, Richard. 1984. "From Fire to Frying Pan: The Impact of Major Power War Involvement on Major Power Dispute Involvement, 1816–1975." *Conflict Management and Peace Science,* 7:71–82.

Thompson, William, and Gary Zuk. 1986. "World Power and the Strategic Trap of Territorial Commitments." *International Studies Quarterly,* 30:249–267.

Touval, Saadia. 1982. *The Peace Brokers: Mediators in the Arab–Israeli Conflict, 1948–1979.* Princeton: Princeton University Press.

Vasquez, John. 1986."Capability, Types of War, Peace." *Western Political Quarterly,* 38:313–327.

———. 1981. *The Power of Power Politics.* New Brunswick, N.J.: Rutgers University Press.

Waltz, Kenneth. 1964. "The Stability of a Bipolar World." *Daedalus,* 93:881–909.

Ward, Michael, and Andrew Kirby. 1987. "Reexamining Spatial Models of International Conflicts." *Annals of the Association of American Geographers,* 77:279–283.

Wayman, Frank. 1982. "War and Power Transitions During Enduring Rivalries." Paper presented at the Institute for the Study of Conflict Theory and International Conflict, Champaign–Urbana.

Weede, Erich. 1975. "World Order in the Fifties and Sixties: Dependence, Deterrence, and Limited Peace." *Peace Science Society (International) Papers,* 24:49–80.

———. 1973. "Nation-Environment Relations as Determinants of Hostilities Among Nations." *Peace Science Society (International) Papers,* 20:67–90.

Wesley, James. 1962. "Frequency of Wars and Geographical Opportunity." *Journal of Conflict Resolution,* 6:387–389.

Wickelgren, Wayne. 1970. "Mutitrace Strength Theory." In *Models of Human Memory*, ed. Donald Norman. New York: Academic Press.

———. 1967. "Exponential Decay and Independence from Irrelevant Associations in Short-Term Recognition Memory for Serial Order." *Journal of Experimental Psychology*, 73:165–171.

Zuk, Gary. 1985. "National Growth and International Conflict: A Reexamination of the Choucri and North Thesis." *Journal of Politics*, 47:269–281.

ABOUT THE AUTHORS

GARY GOERTZ is currently Assistant Professor of Political Science at the University of Florida. He has previously held positions as a Visiting Scholar at the University of Kent and as a Research Associate in the Center for International Economic History at the University of Geneva. He is the author of over a dozen articles on international conflict that have appeared in journals such as *International Studies Quarterly* and the *Journal of Conflict Resolution*.

PAUL F. DIEHL is currently Associate Professor of Political Science and a faculty member in the Program in Arms Control, Disarmament, and International Security at the University of Illinois at Urbana-Champaign. He is the editor or coeditor of *Measuring the Correlates of War* (1990), *The Politics of International Organizations* (1989), and *Through the Straits of Armageddon* (1987) as well as the author of over 30 articles on international conflict.

INDEX

Afghanistan 9, 17
Africa 9, 19, 21, 46, 84–5, 112, 139–40, 144
  see also named countries
Alaska 15
Albania–Yugoslavia disagreements 82, 140
Algeria 16, 21, 58
alliances 11
America, see named areas and countries
Americas, territorial transfers 47, 85
annexation 53–4
Antarctica 24
Arab–Israeli conflict 143
  see also named areas and countries
Argentina 2, 24, 81, 87, 137
Asia, territorial change in 47, 85
  see also named countries
Australia 7
Austria 19, 53
Austro–Hungarian empire 35, 37

Balkan disputes (1912, 1913) 83
Bangladesh 53–4, 137
Beagle Channel 81
Belgium 50, 62, 113
Belize 143
Berlin Conference 46, 51
Biafrans 138
Bolivia 16, 98, 106
borders
  disputes 44, 89, 113
  shared 7, 9–11
  warring 9
boundaries 24
  colonial 9, 19, 82, 85, 140
  ethnic 19, 24, 82, 137
boundary-line disputes 81
Brazil 50
Britain 16, 35, 43, 57, 113, 136–7
  see also United Kingdom
Bulgaria 83

Cambodia 9, 11, 82
Camp David Accord 106

Canada 44, 58, 113
Caribbean 37, 61
Carter administration 14
Central America 37
  see also named countries
cession 53–4
Chad 9, 82, 143
Chile 18, 81, 98, 107
China 11, 19, 37, 50, 86, 113, 136, 139, 143–4
colonial
  boundaries 9, 19, 82, 85, 140
  empires 33
  expansion 99
  powers, dominant 61
colonialism 2, 15–16
  remnants of 140
colonies remaining 133–5
colonization 42
community of nations, influence of 65
Concert of Europe 84, 98–9
conflict
  borders and 7
  diffusion of 8, 11, 26, 124
  ethnic 140
  international 3–27
  interstate 20, 23–5, 83
  measurement of 119
  recurring 20, 25–7, 105–26
    Europe 111
    intercentury differences 111–12
    Middle East 111
    regional distribution of 109, 111–12
    states most involved in 112–13
  research 13
Congress of Vienna 44, 57
conquest 53–4
Correlates of War Project 14, 34
Crimean War 84
Cuba 18
Cyprus 113
Czechoslovakia 50, 85–6, 138

decolonization 37–8, 42, 46, 77, 135
  norm of 23, 65, 78, 130–1, 136–7

175

indicators of 69–71, 75
dependent territories, remaining 133–5
diffusion effect 8–10
diffusion of conflict 26, 124
    effects of alliances 11
    effects of borders 11
    role of geography 8
Dimensions of Nations Project 14
diplomatic time 107
dominant colonial powers 61
domino effect 10

Eastern Europe, reform movement 138
ecological perspective of international relations 3–4
economic pressure, source of territorial expansion 89, 91–2
Egypt 50, 52, 106, 113, 115
El Salvador 7
empires
    Austro-Hungarian 35, 37
    British 33, 35
    colonial 33
    Mongol 2
    Ottoman 35, 37, 62, 85–6, 99, 113, 147
    Portuguese 35
    Roman 2
    Spanish 35
environmental possibilism 4–5
Eritrean rebels 138
Estonia 138
Ethiopia 137–8, 140
Ethiopia–Somalia War 12, 19, 82
ethnic
    boundaries 19, 24, 82, 137
    conflicts 140
    minorities 140
    motivation for territorial expansion 82
    tension 82, 138
Europe 46, 85, 111, 138
    see also named countries
European Community 139
expansionist pressure 89–90, 94, 96, 99, 128, 130, 144
    measurement of 91, 93
expansionist tendencies, measurement of 92

Falkland Islands 2, 24, 137
Falklands dispute 83, 90
Falklands War 52
Fashoda Crisis (1898) 16, 83
Fernando Po 53
Football War 7
France 16, 34, 48, 50, 53, 57, 61–2, 65, 85, 113, 137, 141

General Assembly Resolution 1514 (1960) 23
geographic
    determinism 3
    disputes 24
    proximity 10–11
geography 3
    international relations and 3
    role in the spread of conflict 8
    war and 4–8, 10–12
Germany 19, 37, 43, 48, 50, 53, 86, 99, 113, 118, 140, 147
    reunification 139
    unification 21, 35, 38, 42, 48, 53
Gibraltar 137
Goa 48
Golan Heights 18, 82, 100, 106
government stability 24
Greece 50, 83
Grenada invasion 4
Guatemala 143

hegemony 82
historical claims 19
Hitler 82
homeland territory
    exchanges between states 81–103
        conditions for military conflict 86–90
        spatial distribution 84
        states involved in 85–6
        temporal distribution of 83–4
    transfers 43, 116–17, 132, 140
    military conflict and 86–90
Honduras 7
Hong Kong 135–6
human rights, violation of 23
Hungary 140

imperial empires 33
    see also named empires
imperial/colonial powers, status of
    influence on military conflict 65
    measurement of 68–9, 71
imperial/colonial transfers 43, 57
imperialism 33
independence 21, 23, 44, 51, 53–4, 58, 63
    military conflict and 21–2, 59, 63–6
    LISREL model of 74
    states most involved in 62
    see also national independence
India 2, 20, 35, 48, 50, 53, 85–6, 113, 143–4
India–Pakistan rivalry 47, 83, 90, 105, 113, 124
indigenous forces, correlation with military conflict 64

Index

Indonesia 24
international
  community, restraint imposed by 99,
    128, 131, 137
  conflict, and territory 3–27
  regime 34
  relations
    affected by geography 3
    ecological perspective 3–4
  system 33–4
    changes in the configuration of
      the 140–5
    expansion of the 135–40
    geographic area 35, 38–9
    influence of 65
    measures of size 35
    number of states 35–6, 57
    population 35, 38–9
    regional distribution of states 37
    size of and militarized disputes 42–3
    territorial changes in 38, 40–54
    territorial history 33–56
interstate
  conflicts 20, 23–5, 83
  system 33
    evolution of the 34–8
    territorial changes 43–4
      conditions for military conflict 86–90
      spatial distribution 84
      states involved in 85–6
intrinsic importance of territory 14–17,
    64–6, 88, 122–3, 132–3
  measurement of 66–7, 71, 76, 90–1,
    116, 119–20
Iran 4, 107
Iran–Iraq dispute 143
Iran–Iraq war 52
Iraq 87
Israel 18, 23, 25, 50, 52–3, 57, 82, 85–6,
    100, 106, 113, 115, 124, 144
Italy 21, 50, 86, 113, 147
  unification 21, 35, 38, 42

Japan 37, 50, 86, 99, 106, 113, 143
Jordan 53, 113

Kashmir 113
Korea 19, 34, 83, 139
Kuril Islands 106

lateral pressure 89, 92, 99
Latin America 139
Latvia 138
law of the sea 24
League of Nations 34, 53

mandate system 42, 57
Lebanon 19
Libya 9, 82, 143
LISREL statistical modeling technique
    72–3, 74, 75, 119, 121
Lithuania 38, 138
'long cycle' framework 21
loss-of-strength gradient 4–5, 8
Louisiana Purchase 3, 105

Macedonia 83
major powers 34
  border effect 8
  decline in involvement in territorial
    changes 49
  population size 17
  quest for territory 12–13, 48
  wars 85
Malaysia 24
mandated territory 53–4
market benefits 16
Mauritius 141
mercantilist strategy 16
Mexico 113, 115
Middle East 2, 25, 47, 85, 100, 105,
    111, 141
  see also named areas and countries
militarized disputes
  definition 108
  size of international system and 42–3
  states most involved in 48
military conflict
  conditions for 114–16
  correlation with indigenous forces 64
  frequency of 87
  homeland transfers and 86–90
  interstate territorial changes and 86–90
  national independence and, LISREL
    model 75
  sovereignty and 64–5
  state formation and 57–80
  status of imperial/colonial powers and 65
minorities, ethnic 140
Mongol empire 2
Monroe Doctrine 11
Morocco 50
Mozambique 18

Namibia 135–6
nation-state 34, 36
  definition 33
national independence 44, 58, 63
  growth of 59–60
  and military conflict 21–2, 59, 63–6
    LISREL model of 75

regional distribution 61
  states most involved in 62
national origin 19
nationalist movements 58
nationalist tensions 137–8
Nauru 53
Nazi Germany 19
Netherlands, the 49–50, 61–2
New Caledonia 58, 137
new states 135–40
New Zealand 7
Nicaragua 18
Nigeria 138
nuclear nonproliferation, international standards 131
nuclear weapons, deployment of 18

Ogaden 143
oil embargo (1973) 14
oil reserves 14
opportunity, concept of 5–6, 8
Organization of African Unity 85
Organization of American States 112
Ottoman empire 35, 37, 62, 85–6, 99, 113, 147

Pakistan 2, 9, 50, 86, 113, 143
Palestine 42, 57–8, 106, 133, 138–9
Panama Canal Zone 82
Paraquay 16
People's Republic of China *see* China
Persian Gulf 14
Peru 44
Piedmont 147
plebiscites 117, 144
Poland 36, 43, 50, 85–6, 140
Polish corridor 18, 82
political entity, definition of 40
population
  gains in 16
  pressure for expansion 89, 91–2, 96, 144
Portugal 49–50, 61–2
Portuguese empire 35
power
  decline 128, 130
  measurement of 68–9, 71, 74, 76
  distribution 11, 24, 89–90, 114–15
  see also relative capability distribution
  politics factors 27, 101, 130–1
  transition hypothesis 97
powers
  imperial/colonial 65, 68–9, 71
  major 8, 12–13, 17, 34, 48–9, 85
proximity 10–11
Prussia 86, 147

Puerto Rico 58, 136

race 19
Reagan administration 14
realpolitik
  models 64, 77, 100–1, 130
  view, utility of 128–32
recurring conflict 20, 25–7, 105–26
  Europe 111
  intercentury differences 111–12
  Middle East 111
  regional distribution of 109, 111–12
  states most involved in 112–13
regional hegemony 82
regional integration 139
relational importance of territory 17–21, 64–6, 88, 122–3, 132–3
  ethnic composition of populace 19
  geographic location 17–19
  historical importance 19
  measurement of 67–8, 71, 76, 91, 116, 119–20
relative capabilities, measurement of 92–3, 119–20
relative capability distribution 89, 92–3, 96–7, 99, 123–4, 128–30
  see also power distribution
religion 19
reunification 139
rivalries, enduring 26
  see also India–Pakistan rivalry
Roman Empire 2
Romania 138, 140
Russia 62, 86, 113, 147
  see also Soviet Union

Saar, France's acquisition of the 53
Sakhalin Islands 42
sanctions 23, 136
secession 53–4, 135, 137–8
security 7, 82
separatist movements 58–9
Serbia 83, 147
Seven Weeks War 84
shared borders 7, 9–11
Silesia 140
Sinai Peninsula 106, 115
Six Day War 53, 106
small states, territorial conflict 12
Somalia 12, 19, 82, 140, 143
South Africa 23, 135–6
South America 37, 60–1
  see also named countries
South West African Peoples Organization (SWAPO) 136

Index

sovereign state 33
sovereignty 15–16, 23–5
  functional boundary dispute 24
  military conflict over 64–5
  peaceful surrender of 64
  positional dispute 24
  territorial disputes 24
Soviet–Afghan conflict 9
Soviet Union 12, 17–18, 36, 42–3, 50, 52, 59, 62, 82–3, 85–6, 106, 138, 147
  see also Russia
Spain 25, 44, 48–50, 53, 62, 137
Spanish–American War 25
Spanish empire 35
Sri Lanka 58, 77
state formation and military conflict 20–3, 57–80
  conditions for 62–6
statehood, peaceful transition to 22–3
state-nations 82
states
  involved in homeland transfers 85–6
  involved in independence cases 61–2
  involved in interstate changes 85–6
  involved in militarized disputes 48
  involved in recurrent conflict 113
  involved in territorial changes 47–8, 50
  major power 8, 12–13, 17, 34, 48–9
  new 135–40
  number in the international system 35–6, 57
  regional distribution in the international system 37
  sovereign 33
  Third World 57
structural equation modeling 76
Suedetenland 19, 82
Switzerland 34
Syria 19, 82, 113

Taiwan 139
territory
  acquisition of, disadvantages 20
  changes of 40–1
    1816–1980 147–64
    annexation 53–4
    associated with the World Wars 47, 83–4
    cession 53–4
    conquest 53–4
    frequency of 46
    the future 127–46
    independence granted 53–4
    in the international system 38–54
    interstate 43–4, 86–90
    major powers and 49

  military conflict and 48–9, 51–2
  number of 41
  perceived legitimacy of 114–15, 117–20, 123
  rate of 42
  recurring conflict and 105–26
  secession 53–4
  states involved in 47–8, 50
  unification 53–4
conflict and 3–27
  realpolitik approach 27, 64, 77, 100–1, 128–32
  roots of 2, 24
  small states 12
disputes about 2, 23–4, 140
  current 140–4
  sovereignty and 24
exchange of
  frequency of 84
  legitimacy of, measurement 117–20
expansion of 81, 89
  economic pressure, effect on 89, 91–2
  ethnic motivation 82
  motives 81–2
  population pressure, effect on 89, 91–2, 96, 144
homeland 43, 81–103, 116–17, 132, 140
importance of 93, 96–7, 100, 114–15, 128, 130, 132–6
  intrinsic 14–17, 64–7, 71, 75, 88, 90–1, 116, 119–20, 122–3, 132–3
  measurement of 66–8, 71, 75, 90–1, 116, 119
  relational 17–21, 64–8, 71, 75, 88, 91, 116, 119–20, 122–3, 132–3
international conflict and 3–27
land value 16
mandated 53–4
proximity 8
resource value 15
significance of 1–31
transfers of 43–5, 47, 51
  Africa 46
  Americas 47, 85
  area involved 45–6
  Middle East 47, 85
  population involved 45–6
  temporal distribution 83–4
  terms of 106–7, 115
Third Reich 19
Third World states 57
Togoland 43
trade routes, control over 16
treaties 42, 118, 144
Tromelin Island 141
Turkey 50, 53, 62, 83, 85–6, 147

179

Index

unification 21, 53–4, 139
United Arab Republic 38, 139
United Kingdom 34, 48, 50, 53, 61–2, 65, 113
  see also Britain
United Nations 34, 53
United Nations Charter 23, 131
United States 11, 15, 18, 25, 44, 50, 65, 82–3, 85, 107, 112–13, 115, 137

Versailles Treaty 118
Vietnam 11, 16, 58, 82, 139, 143
Vietnam War 9, 18

war 2–3
  geography and 4–8, 10–12
  spatial diffusion of 9–11
  temporal diffusion of 11
War of Italian Unification 84
War of the Pacific 98, 107
warring borders 9
'war-weariness' hypothesis 25
West Bank 19, 53, 100, 106, 144
West Berlin 83
willingness, concept of 5–6, 8
World War II, watershed 36, 52
World Wars, territorial changes associated with 47, 83–4

Yom Kippur War 115
Yugoslavia 50, 52, 85–6, 138, 147

Zanzibar 127
zones of viability 4